Edition 1 – Transformation

JoySoul Connection

90-Day
Devotional & Daily Planner

Living Everyday
with **Purpose** for the **LORD**

amanda lingle

Trilogy Christian Publishers

A Wholly Owned Subsidiary of Trinity Broadcasting Network

2442 Michelle Drive

Tustin, CA 92780

For information, address Trilogy Christian Publishing
Rights Department, 2442 Michelle Drive, Tustin, Ca 92780.
Trilogy Christian Publishing/ TBN and colophon are trademarks of Trinity Broadcasting Network.
For information about special discounts for bulk purchases, please contact Trilogy Christian Publishing.
Manufactured in the United States of America

10 9 8 7 6 5 4 3 2 1
Library of Congress Cataloging-in-Publication Data is available.
ISBN 979-8-88738-393-4
ISBN 979-8-88738-394-1 (ebook)

Dedication

I dedicate this devotional planner to my Lord and Savior Jesus Christ and all of His chosen that He has called here.

God loves you. God chose you. You are His.

Love,

your sister in Christ,

amanda

Acknowledgements

The *JoySoul Connection Planner* has truly been a labor of love. I want to first thank my Lord and Savior for entrusting me with this work. Without Him, *JoySoul Connection* wouldn't exist.

I would like to extend a special thank you to *my husband, Jason*. You have been so supportive throughout this entire process; my biggest cheerleader, encourager, and prayer warrior. Thank you for your endless love and support. To my kids, *Bradyn and Dylan*: you two have blessed me so much with your prayers and kind words of encouragement when I have shown you my latest updates and edits to the planner. Love you boys.

Mary Anne, Al, and Sara (mom, dad, and sister), you three are my rocks. Thank you for your encouragement and love forever and always.

Tara-Leigh Cobble, we've never met, but I wanted to give you a *special thank you* because *The Bible Recap* enabled me to read the *entire* Bible within one year, better understand the entire Bible story, and grow in my relationship with the Lord, and it opened my eyes and heart to the mission the Lord has placed on my heart. I'm incredibly grateful for you and your obedience to the work God has called you to. Your work has and will forever have a positive impact on my life and on the Kingdom. *Thank you.*

My D-Group ladies: Venessa, Sydney, Beth, Alyssa, Denise, Vickie, Carla, Wendy, Cari, Kristina, Jessica and Jesi, thank you ladies for your support and prayers during the making of the *JoySoul Connection Planner*. The Lord has forever blessed me with this special group and our friendships.

Thank you to *my JoySoul prayer circle group*! In addition to praying with me and encouraging me, these women used the *JoySoul Connection Planner* for five weeks and gave me feedback so that I could better help the users of the planner. *Lynley, Mimi, and Molly,* thank you so much for your help in making valuable tweaks for the *JoySoul Connection Planner Edition 1 – Transformation.*

Jenna, thank you for being the first person to purchase and gift the *JoySoul Connection Planner,* and thank you, Nick, for being the second! Seeing the spark in your eye when you first heard me talk about the Lord placing *JoySoul Connection Planner* on my heart and then your incredible support through the development process have been such precious blessings to my spirit. Thank you for your sweet encouragement and support.

Nicole, you were the very first person to help me connect the dots and see what the Lord was revealing to me regarding the creation of *JoySoul Connection.* Your coaching was so invaluable to the beginning phases of this special work, and I'm so thankful the Lord put us together; it was no accident.

Monica, thank you so much for your invaluable feedback and tweaks to the *JoySoul Connection Planner.* You helped me understand how I could make the introduction pages more valuable for the *JoySoul* readers and the *JoySoul* brand.

Table of Contents

Preface

Hi *JoySoul*,

I'm so glad you're here! I'm honored that God led you to the *JoySoul Connection Devotional and Planner*.

If you find yourself consistently feeling overwhelmed, disorganized, unfulfilled, or discouraged in your daily walk with the Lord, it's no accident you are reading this; the Lord has brought you here.

This devotional planner is designed to take you on a ninety-day journey that will help you become consistent with your quiet time through daily habits, increase your awareness of the Lord's voice, bring you joy, strengthen your prayer life, and accomplish your purpose-driven goals! You will begin feeling clearer, happier, and more connected with the Lord, which will lead to the fruits of the Spirit radiating out in your life.

John 15:5 says, "I am the vine; you are the branches. If you remain in me and I in you, you will bear much fruit; apart from me you can do nothing." The Lord brought me this verse when He placed *JoySoul Connection* on my heart. This verse initially revealed to me why my past had been filled with so much heartache, guilt, shame, and disappointment. With His loving grace, the Lord gave me clear awareness that all the pain from my past was because I wasn't consistently choosing to trust Him; I wasn't submitting to His authority in and over my life.

Through an experience of His transformative power in my life, I came to realize the purpose He laid on my heart: to encourage women to get out of the distraction trap from the enemy and live with purpose every day for the Lord!

I pray that as you utilize this planner God will bring you wisdom, knowledge, and understanding for His call on your life to *live on purpose for His special purpose for you.*

God loves you. God chose you. You are His.

Love,
your sister in Christ,
amanda

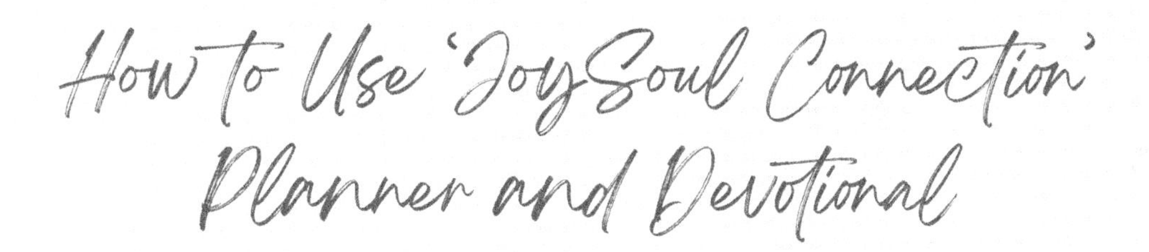

How to Use 'JoySoul Connection' Planner and Devotional

Monthly Page:

"Start with eternity in mind, but most importantly, surrender your intentions, desires, and plans to the Lord."

amanda lingle

"We make our plans, but the LORD determines our steps."

Proverbs 16:9 (KJV)

Utilize this page to set priorities and intentions for the month that align with your goals. This page can also be used as a diary of any special events during the month. *When establishing goals, the method that has best helped me establish clear goals is the SMART acronym method.*

S.M.A.R.T. Specific, Measurable, Achievable, Relevant, and Time-Bound

If you are new to this approach, I recommend starting with *one* goal and then building your goals from there, based upon what God calls you to. This way you can see the progress you are making, re-set, or make tweaks as needed, and avoid overwhelm.

For more information on SMART goal setting, check out my resource pages at the end of this devotional planner.

***Joysoul Connection* Daily Page:**

This is my favorite planner page!

God has revealed to me that to grow in the plans and purposes He has for us, we must ensure we are building our days on a solid foundation that invites Him into the driver's seat.

The story in Luke 6:47-48 sums it up best:

> As for everyone who comes to me and hears my words and puts them into practice, I will show you what they are like. They are like a man building a house, who dug down deep and laid the foundation on the rock. When a flood came, the torrent struck that house but could not shake it, because it was well built.

This page is all about building a strong foundation with the Lord each day through each intention point section. Using the *JoySoul Connection* daily page will enable you to experience daily connection with the Lord, maintain healthy habits, and accomplish your goals! I hope you are as excited as I am to start using this page on the daily!

***JoySoul Connection* Daily Page: Daily Reading**

"It is written: Man shall not live by bread alone, but by every word that comes out of the mouth of God."

Matthew 4:4

If you have not been able to read through the entire Bible yet, I recommend using the daily reading section to set up a daily Bible reading plan.

The resource that helped me do this is a Bible reading plan called *The Bible Recap* by Tara-Leigh Cobble. You can find the link for more information about this Bible reading plan on my resources page in the back of this devotional planner.

If you are like I was and do not understand the Bible, *The Bible Recap* is a total game-changer. I started my first trip through the Bible on August 23, 2020 and finished on August 23, 2021! I also started again in January 2022 for my second round. I truly believe this is part of the *JoySoul Connection* process and why God has called you here. *So, if you haven't read through the Bible yet, this is God's little nudge and wink to make that a priority this year.*

JoySoul Connection Daily Page: Confess

My husband and I like to entertain in the backyard of our home, and we live in Texas, so it gets hot! We always make sure we have the ice machine going, and we keep plenty of water and sodas for our guests and kids. So, as you can imagine, our cooler is a staple at our get-togethers. After one of our events, Texas had a crazy temperature change resulting in a freeze and snow. Our cooler was left outside and out of sight, and consequently, out of mind. I'm embarrassed to say, but that cooler was left out for about two to three weeks, and when I finally realized, I wasn't sure what I would find inside. Sure enough, when I opened the cooler, what once was chilled, clear ice and fresh waters and sodas, was now murky, stinky water, and some of the water and soda cans seemed to start to disintegrate in the water. Girl, it was a mess! And did I say super stinky?

I tell you this story because what happened to the insides of that cooler reminded me of what happens to our hearts when we don't confess, repent, and release the burden of our sin to the Lord.

My friend, it's okay. Please trust me when you read this. The Lord already knows it all. *All* the sins girl, even the ones you don't talk about. First, I want you to know you are not alone. I've been there too, and I have to continue to remind myself that the Lord is safe and will heal me and transform me from the inside out. All I need to do when I slip up is release, surrender, and trust Him to heal me from my sins. The fear of the Lord is our strength. One thing I've started to ask Him for consistently this year is to help me in my weakness when I'm tempted to sin. I know there are just some things I must continue to work through, and I humble my heart to the Lord knowing that His strength is the only power strong enough to help me overcome some of my sinful strongholds.

The enemy wants you to think you can't really be cleaned from sin, that it's just something that needs to stay hidden, or he tries to chain your heart to guilt. Sister, the cross was not yours to bear! Our Lord and Savior picked up our cross, carried it for us, and covers us with His righteous mercy. You are safe in the arms of our Lord and Savior.

My heart is fired up to lovingly encourage you that the Lord has an incredible plan and purpose for your life. One of those is to lift your spirit and remove the weight of the sin you have held onto—either because you have been too afraid to reveal it or because you have struggled to really trust that the Lord has forgiven you. I pray this encourages you to stop holding in that shame of sin and stop believing the enemy's lies that the Lord can't redeem you. Our Lord and Savior truly loves you and gave his life to wash your sin away, cleanse you, and pour out His rich righteousness, mercy, and grace over you.

You are so loved. Please know and remember that. The fact that you are reading this right now is no accident. The Lord wants you to know just how deep His love for you is.

Lord Jesus, I pray over your precious JoySoul *reading this right now. Comfort her heart and reveal to her that You are a safe place for her to lay her burdens down and confess her sin. In Jesus' name, Amen.*

God loves you. God chose you. You are His.

Love,
your sister in Christ,
amanda

JoySoul Daily: Daily Schedule and Daily Action Section

With no goal, there is no change in effort; if you want something to get done, you need to schedule it. Otherwise, that "something" is just a dream, rather than a dream put into action.

I use the schedule section to organize not only my work meetings but also to schedule things like my movement time, my *JoySoul Connection* time, trips to the grocery store, my son's school, practices, etc.

You can use this daily schedule to plan all the essential things you need to do each day. I left the "time" section blank, because we all have different daily schedules. This gives you the ability to lay out your hours exactly how they best fit you.

The "Daily Action List" gives you the ability to narrow down to some specific actions you can do that day to move the needle towards accomplishing your bigger goal. For example, if your goal is to lose two pounds for the week, you could ask yourself what daily action step(s) you need to complete for the day to ensure you will hit your goal by the end of the week.

I find that when we have big goals, we need to be able to break them down into smaller chunks, so they aren't overwhelming. This daily act also allows us to see our progress and celebrate the small wins of the day.

JoySoul Daily: Encourage

According to Max Lucado, to "encourage" means "to inspire with courage, spirit, or hope" (Lucado, "The Power of Encouragement"). To be an encourager is a command from the Lord: "encourage one another and build one another up..." (1 Thessalonians 5:11, ESV).

Fun fact: this section was not originally on the daily page. However, throughout the process of creating this planner, I realized that this section could be one of the more transformative for us as believers as we live out the Lord's commandment to love others.

As you utilize the planner, your senses are going to be awakened to the Lord's presence, He is going to be filling you up with encouragement, and with all the fullness of His love and Spirit, you are going to have so much love and light to share with others. And the Lord will have the ability to use you because of your fullness in Him.

I have included this encouragement section so that each morning, as you set your intentions for the day with the Lord in *JoySoul* daily, you can list out the name of the person you are intending to encourage for the day and the action you will take to provide the encouragement.

I included a space for a second name because I wanted you to have a moment to pray to the Lord to bring you someone to encourage, asking Him to guide you to that exact person. At the end of the day, you can write in whom the Lord led you to and how you provided encouragement.

This could be as easy as a text message, an email, an anonymous handwritten note...however the Lord leads you. This second part may feel uncomfortable on some days because the Lord may call you to someone you don't even know. Whatever the case may be, wherever the Lord leads you, I know this will offer a beautiful opportunity to keep your ears and eyes open to the Lord's voice.

Lord, I pray you would give this JoySoul *comfort and courage as you lead her to be an encourager to others. In Jesus' name, Amen.*

***JoySoul* Daily: Prayers for You and Prayers for Others**

This section of the daily page is one I am very excited about for you as the user of the planner. This prompting will help enrich your prayer life and I know the Lord will bless you and those you pray for through your faithfulness.

The Bible is filled with scriptures on prayer. In the NIV there are 367 Bible verses on prayer. A couple of my favorite Scriptures on prayer are 1 Thessalonians 5:17, which says "pray continually," and Philippians 4:6 (NLT), which says "Don't worry about anything, instead pray about everything. Tell God what you need, and thank him for all that he has done."

The quality of our prayer lives is paramount to the growth in our connections and relationships with the Lord. We also experience the fruit of peace when we make prayer a daily habit.

For more resources on prayer check out my resources section at the back of this planner.

***JoySoul Connection*: Week in Review**

Something I've consistently heard from successful people is that they regularly take time to "think", some even every day. What we can learn from Jesus' life is that he also took time to get away in solitude to think and pray consistently. If our Lord and Savior took time for this, how much more do we need to do this? Use this page as a guide for prayer and reflection. It will help you keep your highest priorities at the forefront. Be honest about what you are prioritizing, and consider whether you should be giving those things less time. I pray God will lead each of you during this reflection and thinking time.

How To Use the *JoySoul Connection Planner*: Overview

The exciting thing is that God brought you here. You did not stumble upon the *JoySoul Connection Devotional Planner* by accident. Something has been keeping you from maintaining a daily awareness of the Lord's presence, and He is calling you back into His loving arms. He has a very special plan and purpose that is intended only for you. The kingdom of heaven needs your special purpose in action.

With that said, don't overthink how to use this planner. Don't be concerned with whether or not you are doing it right or in the way God wants you to. All you need to do is have faith that the Lord will lead you and ask Him to do just that. Ask Him to reveal to you how He wants you to utilize this tool.

He is your comforter and guide through this process. Lean on Him, and He will direct your steps.

I'm so glad you're here, *JoySoul*.

God loves you. God chose you. You are His.

Love,
your sister in Christ,
amanda

Prologue

You Ready, *JoySoul*?

"In the beginning, God created the heavens and the earth."

Genesis 1:1

As you see from God's Word above, creating the foundation of where we live, work, and carry out God's purposes was the very first task the Lord completed. We can apply this same action in our own lives by starting each day with eternity in mind.

What do I mean by eternity? Well, I got this idea when I read Stephen Covey's book *The 7 Habits of Highly Effective People*. The second of the seven habits is "begin with the end in mind" (Covey 1989). What this means is to begin each day, task, or project with a clear vision of your desired direction and destination.

With that said, our foundation of faith and health must be strong so that, with the Lord's help, we can consistently equip ourselves for each day's mission and purpose by beginning with the end—our eternity with Christ—in mind.

Consistently living with eternity in mind prepares us for both dealing with the sufferings that we face while living in a fallen world and living out our eternal mission with our Lord and Savior Jesus Christ.

Think of a few other examples where having a strong foundation is key to the success of a mission, then share your thoughts in the *JoySoul Connection* Facebook group.

I've included some of my own thoughts below.

My first example is building a house. The foundation must come first. However, before the foundation can be laid, the plan to build the house must be completed.

I also think of successful athletes. What is their foundation? Much of their success is rooted in their daily and consistent training. They train, diet, and sleep in ways that enable them to perform at their peak.

So, what does this mean for us as we desire to maintain healthy bodies, minds, and souls?

We need a daily foundation that we can build on to stay in tune with the Lord. We need to invite Him into our plans, allow Him to lead us, and awaken our senses to hear His voice. For we are God's handiwork, created in Christ Jesus to do good works, which God prepared in advance for us to do (Ephesians 2:10).

This is exactly why I created the *JoySoul Connection Planner*. The Lord placed it on my heart to enable His chosen to build strong foundational daily habits to move them away from distraction and into action towards the purposes and plans He has created for them to do. You Ready? Let's do this!

Monthly Planner

SUN	MON	TUES	WED

"For I know the plans I have for you, declares the LORD, plans for welfare and not for evil, to give you a future and a hope."

JEREMIAH 29:11 (ESV)

Month Year

THURS	FRI	SAT

Priority List

Monthly Goals

DEVOTIONAL WEEK 1:

My Transformation Story

"Humble yourselves, therefore, under God's mighty hand, that he may lift you up in due time. Cast all your anxiety on Him because He cares for you."

1 Peter 5:6-7

When I was eight years old, I was baptized. I asked the Lord to come into my life and save me from my sin. At that time, I didn't truly have a grasp on what was next and how walking with God would look in my life, but I did know that I wanted to follow God. In my late teens and college years, I lost my way. I started to live in a way that *I* felt was right. And if God didn't move in a situation the way I wanted Him to, I would move for Him. I didn't know how bad this way of operating was at the time, but I see now that I didn't make a singular decision to take my life's steering wheel from Him, but that I habitually started to take ownership over my life. I had stopped trusting God's goodness. Fast forward to February 2020, when I was asked to give a "My Why" speech at an annual company meeting. I prayed over what I would say and felt the Lord calling me to share my testimony about the Lord's first intervention in my life. This intervention happened in 2009, while I was going through a divorce from my son's father. I was at the lowest point I had ever been.

One night, after I had put my son to bed, I was alone in my room sobbing and crying out to the Lord for help. I told him, "Lord, I don't know how I am going to make it. I'm not making enough money to pay all the bills. How am I going to be able to work, keep our home and care for my son?" Can you guess what the Lord said to me? He reminded me that I was steering my own life and carrying *all* my burdens. He said to me, "Amanda, give your burdens to me—*all of them*. You can trust me to take care of you." You'd think this would have been easy for me to do, but I had developed such a bad habit of steering my own life that I questioned whether He could really take care of me. Fortunately, at that moment I stopped trying to fight the battles I was facing with my own strength and gave them *all*—my doubts, my worries, my fears, and my control—over to God. And guess what, he followed through on His promise to take care of me. Within the next year, I doubled my income, was able to pay the bills, keep our home and keep my son in a quality daycare.... and I met the love of my life, my husband, Jason.

Thirteen years later, on Easter weekend of 2022, I made the decision to rededicate my life to Christ and be baptized again. Some of you may be asking why I decided to be baptized again. Well, after the February 2020 company meeting where I gave my testimony, I felt a mix of emotions. So many people had come up to me after hearing about God's intervention in my life and told me how God spoke to them through my story. God used it to show them what decisions they needed to make in their own lives. When this happened, I felt like a fraud. I had still been wrestling with fully giving my life to the Lord. That night, as I went outside to be alone with my thoughts, there were scatters of storm clouds outstretched across the sky. I looked out at them with tears in my eyes, and I felt the presence of the Lord. I prayed Psalm 51:10 to Him, which says, "Create in me a clean heart, O God, and renew a right spirit within me."

I did not know the journey that would follow that prayer. Not only did we all experience a worldwide pandemic, but that summer I was haunted by a demonic spiritual attack. It caused me to have extreme fear in my own home. After I prayed the Psalm 51:10 prayer, instead of turning to read the

Bible, I naively turned to reading books about angels, thinking that was part of the spiritual journey the Lord was leading me on. What the Lord later awakened me to is that there are many false prophets/false gods trying to steer our souls away from God and rule over our earthly lives. Their intent is to try to steer us off course from the plan and purposes God has for our lives. But God is the *only true God*. He is the Alpha and the Omega; He is the beginning and the end; and Jesus is *the one and only savior*, and the only way to eternal life in Heaven. To have true intimacy with the Lord, we need to spend time with Him—in his Word and in prayer. The Lord led me to resources to help me do this, and through Scripture memory and reading the Bible, the fear I had departed. It no longer has any power over me. Amen! My prayer is that something in my story resonated in your heart and that you know the Lord has a special purpose and plan for your life.

God bless your week ahead.

God loves you. God chose you. You are His.

Love,
your sister in Christ,
amanda

JoySoul Daily

DATE:

S M T W T F S

PRAISES

CONFESS

TOP PRIORITIES

DAILY READING

MOVEMENT

GOAL	ACTUAL

HYDRATION

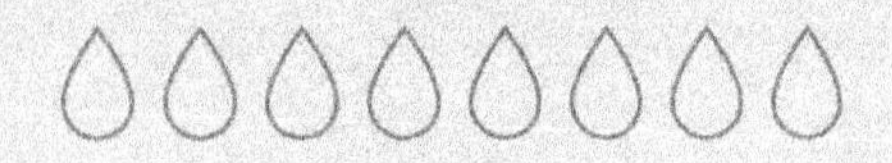

ENCOURAGE

NAME	ACTION
NAME	ACTION

SCHEDULE

TIME	EVENT

DAILY ACTION LIST

SLEEP TRACKER

HOURS GOAL	ACTUAL
BEDTIME	WAKE TIME

PRAYERS FOR ME TODAY

PRAYERS FOR OTHERS TODAY

Notes

JoySoul Daily

DATE:

S M T W T F S

PRAISES

CONFESS

TOP PRIORITIES

DAILY READING

SCHEDULE

TIME	EVENT

DAILY ACTION LIST

MOVEMENT

GOAL	ACTUAL

HYDRATION

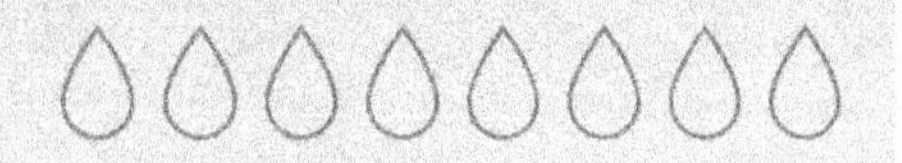

ENCOURAGE

NAME	ACTION
NAME	ACTION

SLEEP TRACKER

HOURS GOAL	ACTUAL
BEDTIME	WAKE TIME

PRAYERS FOR ME TODAY

PRAYERS FOR OTHERS TODAY

Notes

JoySoul Daily

DATE:

S M T W T F S

PRAISES

CONFESS

TOP PRIORITIES

DAILY READING

SCHEDULE

TIME	EVENT

DAILY ACTION LIST

MOVEMENT

GOAL	ACTUAL

HYDRATION

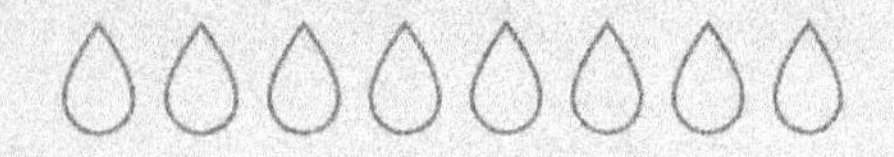

ENCOURAGE

NAME	ACTION
NAME	ACTION

SLEEP TRACKER

HOURS GOAL	ACTUAL
BEDTIME	WAKE TIME

PRAYERS FOR ME TODAY

PRAYERS FOR OTHERS TODAY

Notes

JoySoul Daily

DATE:

S M T W T F S

PRAISES

CONFESS

TOP PRIORITIES

DAILY READING

SCHEDULE

TIME	EVENT

DAILY ACTION LIST

MOVEMENT

GOAL	ACTUAL

HYDRATION

ENCOURAGE

NAME	ACTION
NAME	ACTION

SLEEP TRACKER

HOURS GOAL	ACTUAL
BEDTIME	WAKE TIME

PRAYERS FOR ME TODAY

PRAYERS FOR OTHERS TODAY

Notes

JoySoul Daily

DATE:

S M T W T F S

PRAISES

CONFESS

TOP PRIORITIES

DAILY READING

MOVEMENT

GOAL	ACTUAL

HYDRATION

ENCOURAGE

NAME	ACTION
NAME	ACTION

SCHEDULE

TIME	EVENT

DAILY ACTION LIST

SLEEP TRACKER

HOURS GOAL	ACTUAL
BEDTIME	WAKE TIME

PRAYERS FOR ME TODAY

PRAYERS FOR OTHERS TODAY

Notes

JoySoul Daily

DATE:

S M T W T F S

PRAISES

CONFESS

TOP PRIORITIES

DAILY READING

MOVEMENT

GOAL	ACTUAL

HYDRATION

ENCOURAGE

NAME	ACTION
NAME	ACTION

SCHEDULE

TIME	EVENT

DAILY ACTION LIST

SLEEP TRACKER

HOURS GOAL	ACTUAL
BEDTIME	WAKE TIME

PRAYERS FOR ME TODAY

PRAYERS FOR OTHERS TODAY

Notes

JoySoul Daily

DATE:

S M T W T F S

PRAISES

CONFESS

TOP PRIORITIES

DAILY READING

MOVEMENT

GOAL	ACTUAL

HYDRATION

ENCOURAGE

NAME	ACTION
NAME	ACTION

SCHEDULE

TIME	EVENT

DAILY ACTION LIST

SLEEP TRACKER

HOURS GOAL	ACTUAL
BEDTIME	WAKE TIME

PRAYERS FOR ME TODAY

PRAYERS FOR OTHERS TODAY

Notes

COMMIT TO THE LORD WHATEVER YOU DO AND HE WILL ESTABLISH YOUR PLANS.

PROVERBS 16:3

THE WEEK IN REVIEW .... RATE: ☆☆☆☆☆

SABBATH DAY .... WORD OF THE WEEK ....

REFLECTION WITH THE LORD AND YOUR PRIORITIES

GOD REVEALED TO ME ....

....

THIS WEEK'S BLESSINGS ....

....

WHAT DO I NEED TO SURRENDER TO THE LORD ....

....

PRIORITY PRAYERS FOR MYSELF AND OTHERS

LOOKING AT NEXT WEEK

#1 THING TO DO NEXT ....

EXCUSE TO LET GO OF ....

I AM COMMITING TO THE LORD ....

Sermon & Journal Notes

DEVOTIONAL WEEK 2:

How Do We Recognize God's Voice?

John 15:5 says, "I am the vine; you are the branches. If you remain in me and I in you, you will bear much fruit; apart from me you can do nothing." The Lord brought me this verse when He placed *JoySoul Connection* on my heart. Later, He revealed an analogy to me that helped me better visualize the importance of the truth packed into this verse.

Have you ever struggled to hear or recognize God's voice? Have you looked at decisions through your own worldly thought lens, but then wondered, *where is God in this*? Have you seen other Christians supporting views or not supporting certain views and wondered what God thought about such views?

If you have ever struggled with this, I'm super proud of your reflection and desire to ask, "What does God say?" This is the analogy the Lord brought me: Do you know the book *Where's Waldo*? The character you must search for like crazy to find on the cluttered scene pages?

I have such a hard time finding Waldo when I try. It would be so much easier to spot him if all the scene distractions were removed and it was just him on the page. This made me think of Christians who are trying to hear God's voice or expecting God to show up in their lives but aren't making the time to read their Bibles and *be still with the Lord* (Psalm 46:10). When we miss out on that time, finding the Lord is like trying to find Waldo! We're limiting our ability to be in tune with God, His voice, and His guidance. Be on guard, sister, as this lack of time with the Lord opens our thoughts to the enemy's worldly influences, making it easier to listen to other "voices".

What is one thing you can start doing today to increase your awareness of the Lord's voice? How will you guard your heart from influences that aren't from the Lord? How will you seek guidance to ensure you recognize His promptings?

God bless your week ahead.

God loves you. God chose you. You are His.

Love,
your sister in Christ,
amanda

"I am the vine; you are the branches. If you remain in me and I in you, you will bear much fruit; apart from me, you can do nothing."

John 15:5

JoySoul Daily

DATE:

S M T W T F S

PRAISES

CONFESS

TOP PRIORITIES

DAILY READING

SCHEDULE

TIME	EVENT

DAILY ACTION LIST

MOVEMENT

GOAL	ACTUAL

HYDRATION

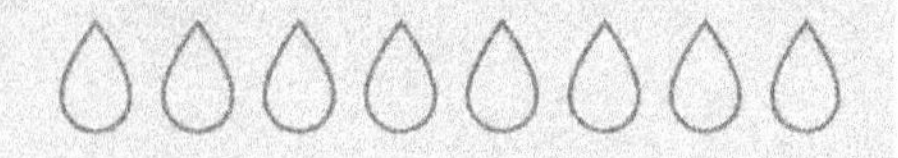

ENCOURAGE

NAME	ACTION
NAME	ACTION

SLEEP TRACKER

HOURS GOAL	ACTUAL
BEDTIME	WAKE TIME

PRAYERS FOR ME TODAY

PRAYERS FOR OTHERS TODAY

Notes

JoySoul Daily

DATE:

S M T W T F S

PRAISES

CONFESS

TOP PRIORITIES

DAILY READING

MOVEMENT

GOAL	ACTUAL

HYDRATION

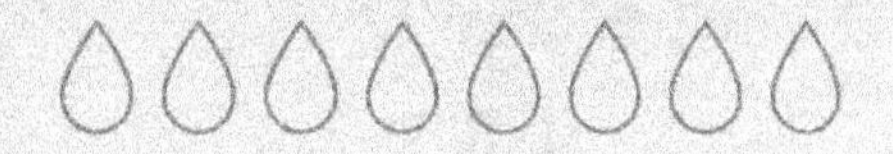

ENCOURAGE

NAME	ACTION
NAME	ACTION

SCHEDULE

TIME	EVENT

DAILY ACTION LIST

SLEEP TRACKER

HOURS GOAL	ACTUAL
BEDTIME	WAKE TIME

PRAYERS FOR ME TODAY

PRAYERS FOR OTHERS TODAY

Notes

JoySoul Daily

DATE:

S M T W T F S

PRAISES

CONFESS

TOP PRIORITIES

DAILY READING

SCHEDULE

TIME	EVENT

DAILY ACTION LIST

MOVEMENT

GOAL	ACTUAL

HYDRATION

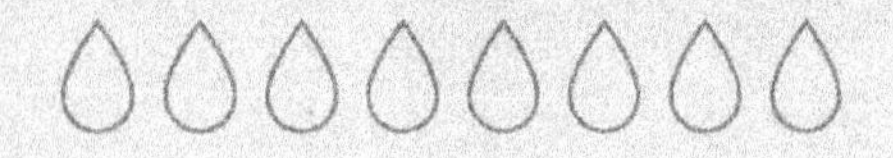

ENCOURAGE

NAME	ACTION
NAME	ACTION

SLEEP TRACKER

HOURS GOAL	ACTUAL
BEDTIME	WAKE TIME

PRAYERS FOR ME TODAY

PRAYERS FOR OTHERS TODAY

Notes

JoySoul Daily

DATE:

S M T W T F S

PRAISES

CONFESS

TOP PRIORITIES

DAILY READING

MOVEMENT

GOAL	ACTUAL

HYDRATION

ENCOURAGE

NAME	ACTION
NAME	ACTION

SCHEDULE

TIME	EVENT

DAILY ACTION LIST

SLEEP TRACKER

HOURS GOAL	ACTUAL
BEDTIME	WAKE TIME

PRAYERS FOR ME TODAY

PRAYERS FOR OTHERS TODAY

Notes

JoySoul Daily

DATE:

S M T W T F S

PRAISES

CONFESS

TOP PRIORITIES

DAILY READING

SCHEDULE

TIME	EVENT

DAILY ACTION LIST

MOVEMENT

GOAL	ACTUAL

HYDRATION

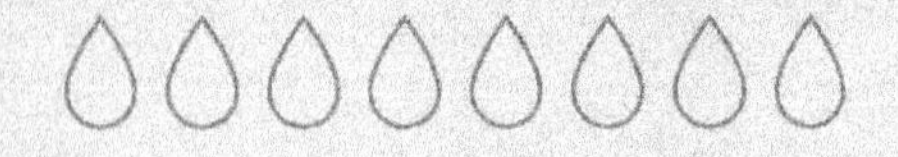

ENCOURAGE

NAME	ACTION
NAME	ACTION

SLEEP TRACKER

HOURS GOAL	ACTUAL
BEDTIME	WAKE TIME

PRAYERS FOR ME TODAY

PRAYERS FOR OTHERS TODAY

Notes

JoySoul Daily

DATE:

S M T W T F S

PRAISES

CONFESS

TOP PRIORITIES

DAILY READING

MOVEMENT

GOAL	ACTUAL

HYDRATION

ENCOURAGE

NAME	ACTION
NAME	ACTION

SCHEDULE

TIME	EVENT

DAILY ACTION LIST

SLEEP TRACKER

HOURS GOAL	ACTUAL
BEDTIME	WAKE TIME

PRAYERS FOR ME TODAY

PRAYERS FOR OTHERS TODAY

Notes

JoySoul Daily

DATE:

S M T W T F S

PRAISES

CONFESS

TOP PRIORITIES

DAILY READING

MOVEMENT

GOAL	ACTUAL

HYDRATION

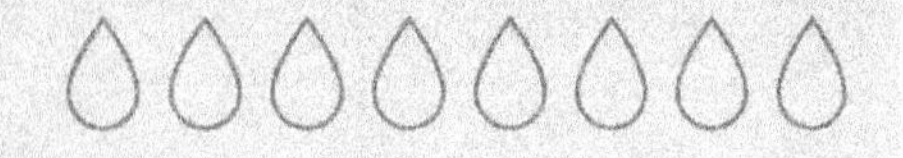

ENCOURAGE

NAME	ACTION
NAME	ACTION

SCHEDULE

TIME	EVENT

DAILY ACTION LIST

SLEEP TRACKER

HOURS GOAL	ACTUAL
BEDTIME	WAKE TIME

PRAYERS FOR ME TODAY

PRAYERS FOR OTHERS TODAY

Notes

COMMIT TO THE LORD WHATEVER YOU DO AND HE WILL ESTABLISH YOUR PLANS.

PROVERBS 16:3

THE WEEK IN REVIEW ______ RATE: ☆ ☆ ☆ ☆ ☆

SABBATH DAY ______ WORD OF THE WEEK ______

REFLECTION WITH THE LORD AND YOUR PRIORITIES

GOD REVEALED TO ME ______

THIS WEEK'S BLESSINGS ______

WHAT DO I NEED TO SURRENDER TO THE LORD ______

PRIORITY PRAYERS FOR MYSELF AND OTHERS

LOOKING AT NEXT WEEK

#1 THING TO DO NEXT ______

EXCUSE TO LET GO OF ______

I AM COMMITING TO THE LORD ______

Sermon & Journal Notes

DEVOTIONAL WEEK 3:

Resurrection in Christ

"Therefore, if anyone is in Christ, he is a new creation. The old has passed away; behold, the new has come."

2 Corinthians 5:17 (ESV)

When I began my journey of writing *JoySoul Connection*, the Lord brought me the beautiful image of a butterfly. I thought about the parallel between a butterfly's life cycle and the redemption and sanctification journey of a follower of Christ. A butterfly starts its life as a caterpillar, and it is attached to a tree. To start the process of becoming a butterfly, it must nourish itself by eating from the leaves of the tree it was placed on. Then, it connects itself to the vine of the tree and turns into a chrysalis. After waiting inside the chrysalis, it is transformed into a beautiful butterfly.

Do you know where I'm going with this? Think about how we start out. When we are born, we are born into sin. Our redemption and sanctification journeys start with reading God's Word, learning about who God is, and feeding our hearts with His truth. Then, when we make the decision to accept Jesus into our hearts and give our lives over to Him, we are transformed into His light bearers.

Just like when butterflies catch the attention of people's eyes when they fly by, I believe we as God's light bearers have the same effect on others. The light and fruit of the Lord's Holy Spirit within us leads them to Christ.

My prayer is that as you spend the next ten weeks in your *JoySoul Connection* planner your joy in the Lord will increase, your heart will have peace, and you will share your joy in Christ with others.

God bless your week ahead.

God loves you. God chose you. You are His.

Love,
your sister in Christ,
amanda

JoySoul Daily

DATE:

S M T W T F S

PRAISES

CONFESS

TOP PRIORITIES

DAILY READING

SCHEDULE

TIME	EVENT

DAILY ACTION LIST

MOVEMENT

GOAL	ACTUAL

HYDRATION

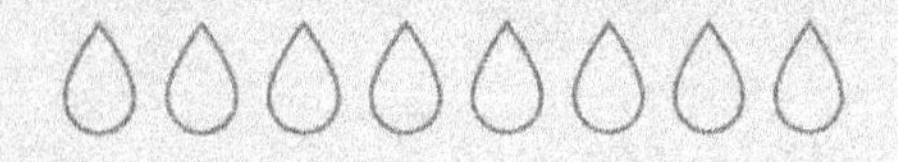

ENCOURAGE

NAME	ACTION
NAME	ACTION

SLEEP TRACKER

HOURS GOAL	ACTUAL
BEDTIME	WAKE TIME

PRAYERS FOR ME TODAY

PRAYERS FOR OTHERS TODAY

Notes

JoySoul Daily

DATE:

S M T W T F S

PRAISES

CONFESS

TOP PRIORITIES

DAILY READING

SCHEDULE

TIME	EVENT

DAILY ACTION LIST

MOVEMENT

GOAL	ACTUAL

HYDRATION

ENCOURAGE

NAME	ACTION
NAME	ACTION

SLEEP TRACKER

HOURS GOAL	ACTUAL
BEDTIME	WAKE TIME

PRAYERS FOR ME TODAY

PRAYERS FOR OTHERS TODAY

Notes

JoySoul Daily

DATE:

S M T W T F S

PRAISES

CONFESS

TOP PRIORITIES

DAILY READING

SCHEDULE

TIME	EVENT

DAILY ACTION LIST

MOVEMENT

GOAL	ACTUAL

HYDRATION

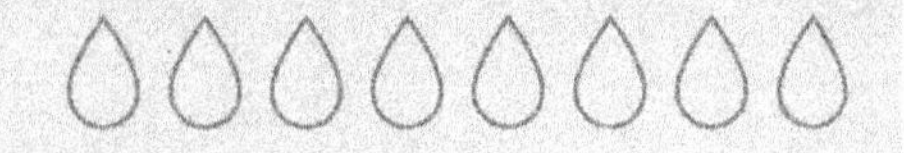

ENCOURAGE

NAME	ACTION
NAME	ACTION

SLEEP TRACKER

HOURS GOAL	ACTUAL
BEDTIME	WAKE TIME

PRAYERS FOR ME TODAY

PRAYERS FOR OTHERS TODAY

Notes

JoySoul Daily

DATE:

S M T W T F S

PRAISES

CONFESS

TOP PRIORITIES

DAILY READING

SCHEDULE

TIME	EVENT

DAILY ACTION LIST

MOVEMENT

GOAL	ACTUAL

HYDRATION

ENCOURAGE

NAME	ACTION
NAME	ACTION

SLEEP TRACKER

HOURS GOAL	ACTUAL
BEDTIME	WAKE TIME

PRAYERS FOR ME TODAY

PRAYERS FOR OTHERS TODAY

Notes

JoySoul Daily

DATE:

S M T W T F S

PRAISES

CONFESS

TOP PRIORITIES

DAILY READING

MOVEMENT

GOAL	ACTUAL

HYDRATION

ENCOURAGE

NAME	ACTION
NAME	ACTION

SCHEDULE

TIME	EVENT

DAILY ACTION LIST

SLEEP TRACKER

HOURS GOAL	ACTUAL
BEDTIME	WAKE TIME

PRAYERS FOR ME TODAY

PRAYERS FOR OTHERS TODAY

Notes

JoySoul Daily

DATE:

S M T W T F S

PRAISES

CONFESS

TOP PRIORITIES

DAILY READING

SCHEDULE

TIME	EVENT

DAILY ACTION LIST

MOVEMENT

GOAL	ACTUAL

HYDRATION

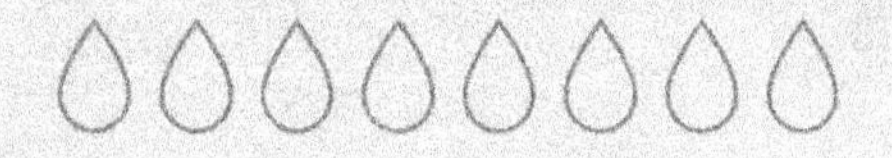

ENCOURAGE

NAME	ACTION
NAME	ACTION

SLEEP TRACKER

HOURS GOAL	ACTUAL
BEDTIME	WAKE TIME

PRAYERS FOR ME TODAY

PRAYERS FOR OTHERS TODAY

Notes

JoySoul Daily

DATE:

S M T W T F S

PRAISES

CONFESS

TOP PRIORITIES

DAILY READING

MOVEMENT

GOAL	ACTUAL

HYDRATION

ENCOURAGE

NAME	ACTION
NAME	ACTION

SCHEDULE

TIME	EVENT

DAILY ACTION LIST

SLEEP TRACKER

HOURS GOAL	ACTUAL
BEDTIME	WAKE TIME

PRAYERS FOR ME TODAY

PRAYERS FOR OTHERS TODAY

Notes

COMMIT TO THE LORD WHATEVER YOU DO AND HE WILL ESTABLISH YOUR PLANS.

PROVERBS 16:3

THE WEEK IN REVIEW .... RATE: ☆ ☆ ☆ ☆ ☆

SABBATH DAY .... WORD OF THE WEEK ....

REFLECTION WITH THE LORD AND YOUR PRIORITIES

GOD REVEALED TO ME ....

....

THIS WEEK'S BLESSINGS ....

....

WHAT DO I NEED TO SURRENDER TO THE LORD ....

....

PRIORITY PRAYERS FOR MYSELF AND OTHERS

LOOKING AT NEXT WEEK

#1 THING TO DO NEXT ....

EXCUSE TO LET GO OF ....

I AM COMMITING TO THE LORD ....

Sermon & Journal Notes

DEVOTIONAL WEEK 4:

Guard Your Heart from False Prophets

"Be on guard against false prophets; they come to you looking like sheep on the outside, but on the inside, they are really like wild wolves. You will know them by what they do. Thorn bushes do not bear grapes, and briers do not bear figs. A healthy tree bears good fruit, but a poor tree bears bad fruit. A healthy tree cannot bear bad fruit, and a poor tree cannot bear good fruit. And any tree that does not bear good fruit is cut down and thrown into the fire. So then, you will know the false prophets by what they do."

Matthew 7:15-20 (GNB)

As you are on your faith journey with the Lord, the enemy will try to steer you away from God's Word and toward the false prophets in the world.

On the outside, they can appear like they have good intentions, some even speak about the Lord and about their love for others, are kind, and will even say they will pray for you. What you must stand on guard against is moving in any direction other than toward the gospel and God's Word.

When I started my rededication to the Lord, I was led astray by a false prophet. She spoke about love, angels, prayer, and healing, but she never spoke about the gospel. At first, it didn't resonate that what I was doing was dangerous, but eventually a lack of peace in my heart began. I kept questioning why she wasn't talking about the saving grace of Jesus.

Unfortunately, I kept engaging in her books and even attended a webinar she led. Shortly after the webinar, the demonic attacks began. They were in the form of extreme fear.

I would physically shake from fear in my own home. I would have night terrors; I couldn't sleep through the night, and I felt helpless. Thankfully the Lord blessed me with access to a biblical counselor, and he led me to Ephesians 6:10-18, the passage about the armor of God. I realized I needed to stay in God's Word to fight the spiritual battle I was facing.

The Lord led me to a resource called *The Bible Recap* by Tara-Leigh Cobble. It is a chronological Bible reading plan with a commentary on each day's reading. I had never been able to read the entire Bible before, but with the help of this resource, I did. This year (2022), I'm reading through the entire Bible for the second time! Praise the Lord; Glory be to God!

After I started reading the Bible, the attacks were still present, but the Word helped me redirect my thoughts. I joined a Bible study called D-Group, and one of the weekly assignments is memorizing scripture. At first, this scared me. I was terrible at memorization and wasn't sure that I could even do it, but they provided so many helpful tips. One of these was putting the memory verse into song form, and that was the key for me. From that point forward, when the night terrors would come, I would say my memory verse, and they would immediately stop! Yes, and amen!

If you are facing a similar situation, the first thing I want to encourage you to do is pray and read your Bible. There are many resources on the UVersion app as well. If you are interested in *The Bible Recap,* check out the Resources: My Faith Favorites page at the back of this devotional planner.

My prayer is that if you haven't already, you will find a Bible reading plan and start your journey through the entire Bible this year!

God bless your week ahead.

God loves you. God chose you. You are His.

Love,

your sister in Christ,

amanda

JoySoul Daily

DATE:

S M T W T F S

PRAISES

CONFESS

TOP PRIORITIES

DAILY READING

MOVEMENT

GOAL	ACTUAL

HYDRATION

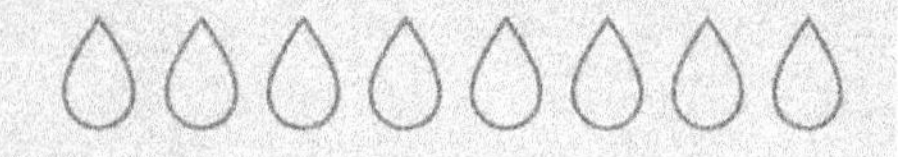

ENCOURAGE

NAME	ACTION
NAME	ACTION

SCHEDULE

TIME	EVENT

DAILY ACTION LIST

SLEEP TRACKER

HOURS GOAL	ACTUAL
BEDTIME	WAKE TIME

PRAYERS FOR ME TODAY

PRAYERS FOR OTHERS TODAY

Notes

JoySoul Daily

DATE:

S M T W T F S

PRAISES

CONFESS

TOP PRIORITIES

DAILY READING

SCHEDULE

TIME	EVENT

DAILY ACTION LIST

MOVEMENT

GOAL	ACTUAL

HYDRATION

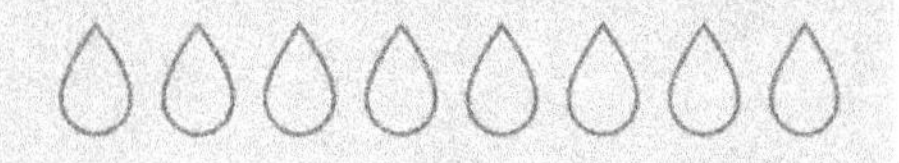

ENCOURAGE

NAME	ACTION
NAME	ACTION

SLEEP TRACKER

HOURS GOAL	ACTUAL
BEDTIME	WAKE TIME

PRAYERS FOR ME TODAY

PRAYERS FOR OTHERS TODAY

Notes

JoySoul Daily

DATE:

S M T W T F S

PRAISES

CONFESS

TOP PRIORITIES

DAILY READING

SCHEDULE

TIME	EVENT

DAILY ACTION LIST

MOVEMENT

GOAL	ACTUAL

HYDRATION

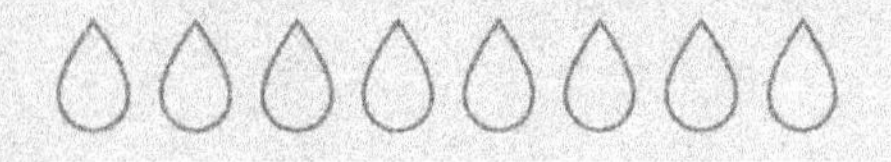

ENCOURAGE

NAME	ACTION
NAME	ACTION

SLEEP TRACKER

HOURS GOAL	ACTUAL
BEDTIME	WAKE TIME

PRAYERS FOR ME TODAY

PRAYERS FOR OTHERS TODAY

Notes

JoySoul Daily

DATE:

S M T W T F S

PRAISES

CONFESS

TOP PRIORITIES

DAILY READING

SCHEDULE

TIME	EVENT

DAILY ACTION LIST

MOVEMENT

GOAL	ACTUAL

HYDRATION

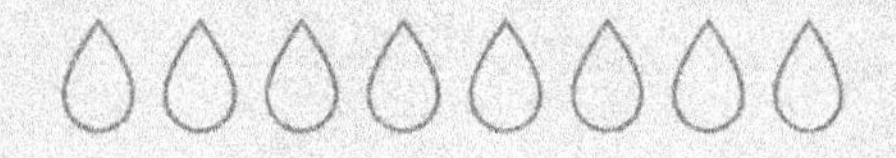

ENCOURAGE

NAME	ACTION
NAME	ACTION

SLEEP TRACKER

HOURS GOAL	ACTUAL
BEDTIME	WAKE TIME

PRAYERS FOR ME TODAY

PRAYERS FOR OTHERS TODAY

Notes

JoySoul Daily

DATE:

S M T W T F S

PRAISES

CONFESS

TOP PRIORITIES

DAILY READING

SCHEDULE

TIME	EVENT

DAILY ACTION LIST

MOVEMENT

GOAL	ACTUAL

HYDRATION

ENCOURAGE

NAME	ACTION
NAME	ACTION

SLEEP TRACKER

HOURS GOAL	ACTUAL
BEDTIME	WAKE TIME

PRAYERS FOR ME TODAY

PRAYERS FOR OTHERS TODAY

Notes

JoySoul Daily

DATE:

S M T W T F S

PRAISES

CONFESS

TOP PRIORITIES

DAILY READING

MOVEMENT

GOAL	ACTUAL

HYDRATION

ENCOURAGE

NAME	ACTION
NAME	ACTION

SCHEDULE

TIME	EVENT

DAILY ACTION LIST

SLEEP TRACKER

HOURS GOAL	ACTUAL
BEDTIME	WAKE TIME

PRAYERS FOR ME TODAY

PRAYERS FOR OTHERS TODAY

Notes

JoySoul Daily

DATE:

S M T W T F S

PRAISES

CONFESS

TOP PRIORITIES

DAILY READING

SCHEDULE

TIME	EVENT

DAILY ACTION LIST

MOVEMENT

GOAL	ACTUAL

HYDRATION

ENCOURAGE

NAME	ACTION
NAME	ACTION

SLEEP TRACKER

HOURS GOAL	ACTUAL
BEDTIME	WAKE TIME

PRAYERS FOR ME TODAY

PRAYERS FOR OTHERS TODAY

Notes

COMMIT TO THE LORD WHATEVER YOU DO AND HE WILL ESTABLISH YOUR PLANS.

PROVERBS 16:3

THE WEEK IN REVIEW .... RATE: ☆☆☆☆☆

SABBATH DAY .... WORD OF THE WEEK ....

REFLECTION WITH THE LORD AND YOUR PRIORITIES

GOD REVEALED TO ME ....

....

THIS WEEK'S BLESSINGS ....

....

WHAT DO I NEED TO SURRENDER TO THE LORD ....

....

PRIORITY PRAYERS FOR MYSELF AND OTHERS

LOOKING AT NEXT WEEK

#1 THING TO DO NEXT ....

EXCUSE TO LET GO OF ....

I AM COMMITING TO THE LORD ....

Sermon & Journal Notes

Monthly Planner

SUN	MON	TUES	WED

"And we know that in all things God works for the good of those who love him, who are called according to his purpose."

ROMANS 8:28

Month Year

THURS	FRI	SAT

Priority List

Monthly Goals

DEVOTIONAL WEEK 5:

You Were Made on Purpose for His Purpose

"And it shall come to pass that everyone who calls upon the name of the LORD shall be saved"

Acts 2:21 (ESV)

When the Lord put *JoySoul* on my heart, He told me, "I want you to make a planner for my distracted chosen. They need Me in their life, and they have important plans that need to be fulfilled. They need to be reminded of the great love I have for them and the special purposes I have for their lives. Where I have them planted at this very moment is no accident."

I'm going to drop some tough truth on you, and please know this is coming from a heart of love for those that the Lord is calling to read this. *If you expect the Lord to work in your life, He can't be in the background of your life*.... meditate on that for a second.

You must be in tune with Him to recognize his voice.

This planner will help you build habits that will lead to growth in your relationship with God, including giving Him the firstfruits of your time, giving Him permission to work in your life, and trusting Him with all the details.

Today, I encourage you to pray the prayer below, which is a take from Psalm 51:1-13:

> *Have mercy on me, O God, according to Your unfailing love, according to Your great compassion blot out my transgressions. Wash away all my iniquity and cleanse*

me from my sin. For I know my transgressions, and my sin is always before me. Against You have I sinned and done what's evil in Your sight, so that You're proved right when You speak and justified when You judge. Surely, I've been a sinner from birth, sinful from the time my mother conceived me. Cleanse me with hyssop, and I'll be clean, wash me, and I'll be whiter than snow. Create in me a pure heart, O God, and renew a steadfast spirit within me. Do not cast me from Your presence or take Your Holy Spirit from me. Restore to me the joy of Your salvation and grant me a willing spirit to sustain me. Then will I teach transgressors Your ways, and sinners will turn back to You. In Jesus' Name I pray. Amen.

You were made on purpose for his purposes.

My prayer is that this message reminds you of the call the Lord has for you and encourages you that He can and will use you where you are planted right now. I pray that you would be filled with the Holy Spirit and remember to walk in step with the Lord every day. Trust Him to carry you through the hard days, and know that He doesn't expect perfection; He just wants your heart.

God bless your week ahead.

God loves you. God chose you. You are His.

Love,
your sister in Christ,
amanda

JoySoul Daily

DATE:

S M T W T F S

PRAISES

CONFESS

TOP PRIORITIES

DAILY READING

MOVEMENT

GOAL	ACTUAL

HYDRATION

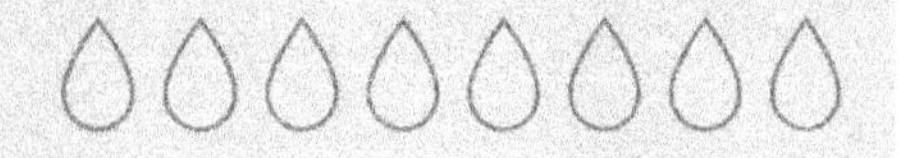

ENCOURAGE

NAME	ACTION
NAME	ACTION

SCHEDULE

TIME	EVENT

DAILY ACTION LIST

SLEEP TRACKER

HOURS GOAL	ACTUAL
BEDTIME	WAKE TIME

PRAYERS FOR ME TODAY

PRAYERS FOR OTHERS TODAY

Notes

JoySoul Daily

DATE:

S M T W T F S

PRAISES

CONFESS

TOP PRIORITIES

DAILY READING

MOVEMENT

GOAL	ACTUAL

HYDRATION

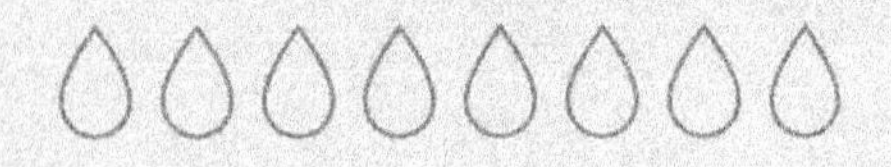

ENCOURAGE

NAME	ACTION
NAME	ACTION

SCHEDULE

TIME	EVENT

DAILY ACTION LIST

SLEEP TRACKER

HOURS GOAL	ACTUAL
BEDTIME	WAKE TIME

PRAYERS FOR ME TODAY

PRAYERS FOR OTHERS TODAY

Notes

JoySoul Daily

DATE:

S M T W T F S

PRAISES

CONFESS

TOP PRIORITIES

DAILY READING

MOVEMENT

GOAL	ACTUAL

HYDRATION

ENCOURAGE

NAME	ACTION
NAME	ACTION

SCHEDULE

TIME	EVENT

DAILY ACTION LIST

SLEEP TRACKER

HOURS GOAL	ACTUAL
BEDTIME	WAKE TIME

PRAYERS FOR ME TODAY

PRAYERS FOR OTHERS TODAY

Notes

JoySoul Daily

DATE:

S M T W T F S

PRAISES

CONFESS

TOP PRIORITIES

DAILY READING

MOVEMENT

GOAL	ACTUAL

HYDRATION

ENCOURAGE

NAME	ACTION
NAME	ACTION

SCHEDULE

TIME	EVENT

DAILY ACTION LIST

SLEEP TRACKER

HOURS GOAL	ACTUAL
BEDTIME	WAKE TIME

PRAYERS FOR ME TODAY

PRAYERS FOR OTHERS TODAY

Notes

JoySoul Daily

DATE:

S M T W T F S

PRAISES

CONFESS

TOP PRIORITIES

DAILY READING

MOVEMENT

GOAL	ACTUAL

HYDRATION

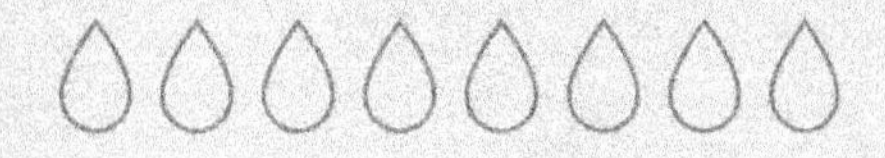

ENCOURAGE

NAME	ACTION
NAME	ACTION

SCHEDULE

TIME	EVENT

DAILY ACTION LIST

SLEEP TRACKER

HOURS GOAL	ACTUAL
BEDTIME	WAKE TIME

PRAYERS FOR ME TODAY

PRAYERS FOR OTHERS TODAY

Notes

JoySoul Daily

DATE:

S M T W T F S

PRAISES

CONFESS

TOP PRIORITIES

DAILY READING

MOVEMENT

GOAL	ACTUAL

HYDRATION

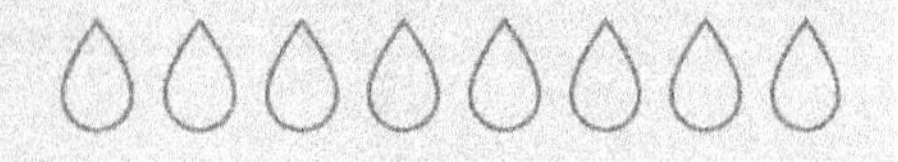

ENCOURAGE

NAME	ACTION
NAME	ACTION

SCHEDULE

TIME	EVENT

DAILY ACTION LIST

SLEEP TRACKER

HOURS GOAL	ACTUAL
BEDTIME	WAKE TIME

PRAYERS FOR ME TODAY

PRAYERS FOR OTHERS TODAY

Notes

JoySoul Daily

DATE:

S M T W T F S

PRAISES

CONFESS

TOP PRIORITIES

DAILY READING

MOVEMENT

GOAL	ACTUAL

HYDRATION

ENCOURAGE

NAME	ACTION
NAME	ACTION

SCHEDULE

TIME	EVENT

DAILY ACTION LIST

SLEEP TRACKER

HOURS GOAL	ACTUAL
BEDTIME	WAKE TIME

PRAYERS FOR ME TODAY

PRAYERS FOR OTHERS TODAY

Notes

COMMIT TO THE LORD WHATEVER YOU DO AND HE WILL ESTABLISH YOUR PLANS.

PROVERBS 16:3

THE WEEK IN REVIEW .... RATE: ☆ ☆ ☆ ☆ ☆

SABBATH DAY .... WORD OF THE WEEK ....

REFLECTION WITH THE LORD AND YOUR PRIORITIES

GOD REVEALED TO ME ....

THIS WEEK'S BLESSINGS ....

WHAT DO I NEED TO SURRENDER TO THE LORD ....

PRIORITY PRAYERS FOR MYSELF AND OTHERS

LOOKING AT NEXT WEEK

#1 THING TO DO NEXT ....

EXCUSE TO LET GO OF ....

I AM COMMITING TO THE LORD ....

Sermon & Journal Notes

DEVOTIONAL WEEK 6:

The Nearness of the Lord

"The people are bringing more than enough for doing the work the Lord commanded to be done."

Exodus 36:5

"The Israelites had done all the work just as the Lord had commanded Moses. Moses inspected the work and saw that they had done it just as the Lord had commanded. So Moses blessed them."

Exodus 39:42-43

As I was reading through Exodus 36-39, I noticed how these chapters reflected the stunning beauty of obedience as God's people built the tabernacle. The people were bringing more than what was needed, and the best craftsmen were using their giftedness to help add to the beauty of the tabernacle. Then, as the work was completed, Moses blessed them, because they had done the work just as the Lord commanded.

Prior to the building of the tabernacle, the Israelites were consistently having difficulty maintaining trust in the Lord's plan for them. Even after He brought them out of slavery and freed them from the oppression of the Egyptians, and even though the Lord was right there with them day and night, the challenges they faced in the desert seemed to easily throw their faith off course.

The fact is that the Lord is always near. However, it's easy for us to forget this when we aren't intentionally spending time with the Lord to renew our minds and guard our hearts.

Are you currently feeling unfulfilled in your season of life?

Are you feeling like something is missing? Are you missing that feeling of connecting within your heart and soul with the Lord?

Or, maybe you're on fire for the Lord, but you don't know what your purpose is. Maybe you're wondering how God can use you if you're not a preacher or a missionary. Maybe you're asking: "What has God called me to? What is my purpose?"

Even if you don't have clarity regarding where you are right now, the fact that you are reading this devotional and putting time into using this planner *is not an accident*. God has called you here. Your life has rich, unique meaning and purpose.

Even amidst the waiting and the questions, when you walk in obedience to the Lord, you enable yourself to receive blessing over your life.

My prayer for you this week is that your heart would be opened to the truths that the Lord is always with you, He sees you, He hears your prayers, and He dearly loves you.

God bless your week ahead.

God loves you. God chose you. You are His.

Love,
your sister in Christ,
amanda

JoySoul Daily

DATE:

S M T W T F S

PRAISES

CONFESS

TOP PRIORITIES

DAILY READING

SCHEDULE

TIME	EVENT

DAILY ACTION LIST

MOVEMENT

GOAL	ACTUAL

HYDRATION

ENCOURAGE

NAME	ACTION
NAME	ACTION

SLEEP TRACKER

HOURS GOAL	ACTUAL
BEDTIME	WAKE TIME

PRAYERS FOR ME TODAY

PRAYERS FOR OTHERS TODAY

Notes

JoySoul Daily

DATE:

S M T W T F S

PRAISES

CONFESS

TOP PRIORITIES

DAILY READING

SCHEDULE

TIME	EVENT

DAILY ACTION LIST

MOVEMENT

GOAL	ACTUAL

HYDRATION

ENCOURAGE

NAME	ACTION
NAME	ACTION

SLEEP TRACKER

HOURS GOAL	ACTUAL
BEDTIME	WAKE TIME

PRAYERS FOR ME TODAY

PRAYERS FOR OTHERS TODAY

Notes

JoySoul Daily

DATE:

S M T W T F S

PRAISES

CONFESS

TOP PRIORITIES

DAILY READING

SCHEDULE

TIME	EVENT

DAILY ACTION LIST

MOVEMENT

GOAL	ACTUAL

HYDRATION

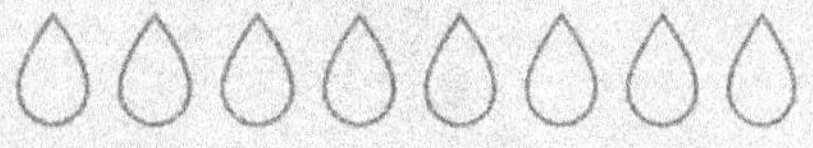

ENCOURAGE

NAME	ACTION
NAME	ACTION

SLEEP TRACKER

HOURS GOAL	ACTUAL
BEDTIME	WAKE TIME

PRAYERS FOR ME TODAY

PRAYERS FOR OTHERS TODAY

Notes

JoySoul Daily

DATE:

S M T W T F S

PRAISES

CONFESS

TOP PRIORITIES

DAILY READING

MOVEMENT

GOAL	ACTUAL

HYDRATION

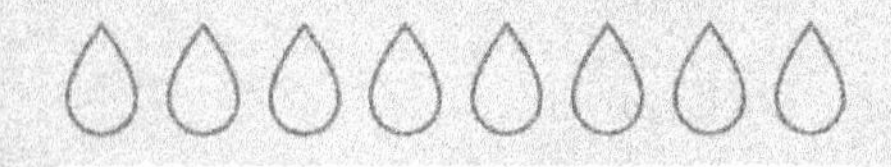

ENCOURAGE

NAME	ACTION
NAME	ACTION

SCHEDULE

TIME	EVENT

DAILY ACTION LIST

SLEEP TRACKER

HOURS GOAL	ACTUAL
BEDTIME	WAKE TIME

PRAYERS FOR ME TODAY

PRAYERS FOR OTHERS TODAY

Notes

JoySoul Daily

DATE:

S M T W T F S

PRAISES

CONFESS

TOP PRIORITIES

DAILY READING

SCHEDULE

TIME	EVENT

DAILY ACTION LIST

MOVEMENT

GOAL	ACTUAL

HYDRATION

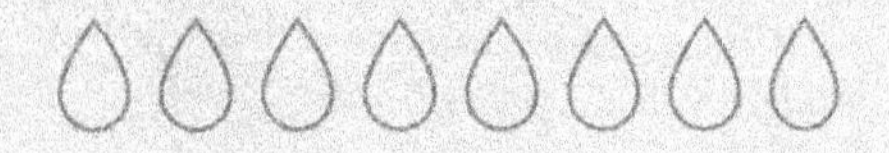

ENCOURAGE

NAME	ACTION
NAME	ACTION

SLEEP TRACKER

HOURS GOAL	ACTUAL
BEDTIME	WAKE TIME

PRAYERS FOR ME TODAY

PRAYERS FOR OTHERS TODAY

Notes

JoySoul Daily

DATE:

S M T W T F S

PRAISES

CONFESS

TOP PRIORITIES

DAILY READING

SCHEDULE

TIME	EVENT

DAILY ACTION LIST

MOVEMENT

GOAL	ACTUAL

HYDRATION

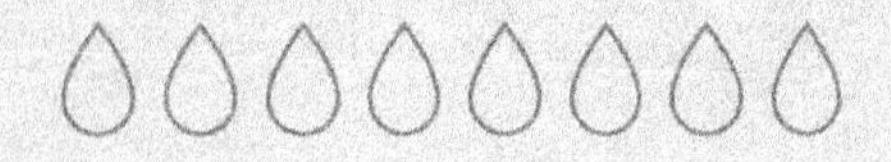

ENCOURAGE

NAME	ACTION
NAME	ACTION

SLEEP TRACKER

HOURS GOAL	ACTUAL
BEDTIME	WAKE TIME

PRAYERS FOR ME TODAY

PRAYERS FOR OTHERS TODAY

Notes

JoySoul Daily

DATE:

S M T W T F S

PRAISES

CONFESS

TOP PRIORITIES

DAILY READING

MOVEMENT

GOAL	ACTUAL

HYDRATION

ENCOURAGE

NAME	ACTION
NAME	ACTION

SCHEDULE

TIME	EVENT

DAILY ACTION LIST

SLEEP TRACKER

HOURS GOAL	ACTUAL
BEDTIME	WAKE TIME

PRAYERS FOR ME TODAY

PRAYERS FOR OTHERS TODAY

Notes

COMMIT TO THE LORD WHATEVER YOU DO AND HE WILL ESTABLISH YOUR PLANS.

PROVERBS 16:3

THE WEEK IN REVIEW .... RATE: ☆☆☆☆☆

SABBATH DAY .... WORD OF THE WEEK ....

REFLECTION WITH THE LORD AND YOUR PRIORITIES

GOD REVEALED TO ME ....

....

THIS WEEK'S BLESSINGS ....

....

WHAT DO I NEED TO SURRENDER TO THE LORD ....

....

PRIORITY PRAYERS FOR MYSELF AND OTHERS

LOOKING AT NEXT WEEK

#1 THING TO DO NEXT ....

EXCUSE TO LET GO OF ....

I AM COMMITING TO THE LORD ....

Sermon & Journal Notes

DEVOTIONAL WEEK 7:

Your Inner Circle

"The angel of the Lord went up from Gilgal to Bochim and said, "I brought you up out of Egypt and led you into the land I swore to give to your ancestors. I said, 'I will never break my covenant with you, and you shall not make a covenant with the people of this land, but you shall break down their altars.' Yet you have disobeyed me. Why have you done this? And I have also said, 'I will not drive them out before you; they will become traps for you, and their gods will become snares to you.'"

Judges 2:1-3

In the world of social media, we are flooded with false images, comparisons, judgments, and trends that don't reflect the values of being a believer and follower of Jesus. As I was reading through *The Bible Recap* chronological reading plan and listening to Cobble's commentary on the book of Judges, I realized the Lord provided an example of the serious impact that this can have on believers.

Israel finally came into the promised land, but instead of ensuring they drove out the Canaanites from their land (as the Lord had commanded), they settled with them. Think about that for a second. Why would they even entertain this idea after the warnings and commands the Lord had given?

The Israelites had just come out of the desert, and their parents had been oppressed as slaves by Egyptian rulers, yet instead of trusting the Lord's command, they allowed themselves to be enticed by the sophisticated outward appearance of the Canaanites.

However, they didn't initially see the wicked hearts of

the Canaanite people, who engaged in child sacrifice and other obscene forms of worship to false gods. The Israelites' disobedience had catastrophic effects that led them down a very dark path.

Have you ever felt a nudge from the Lord not to engage in a certain friendship or relationship? Are you currently in such a situation?

I want to encourage you that when you trust the Lord, He will guard your heart and provide protection. As He promises in Proverbs 3:5-6, "Trust in the LORD with all your heart, and do not lean on your own understanding. In all your ways acknowledge him, and he will make straight your paths" (ESV).

We most likely haven't had the opportunity to meet. If I can't speak these words over you in person, my prayer is that you know the Lord loves you very much. The Lord has great plans and purposes for your life.

If you sense His Holy Spirit warning you not to engage in a relationship, friendship, or whatever that "thing" is for you, I want you to hear this from me today, as your sister in Christ, and part of the body of Christ: I'm in your inner circle, and I am praying that you will make the decision to put your trust in the Lord and follow His lead in the situation. You can trust Him.

God bless your week ahead.

God loves you. God chose you. You are His.

Love,

your sister in Christ,

amanda

JoySoul Daily

DATE:

S M T W T F S

PRAISES

CONFESS

TOP PRIORITIES

DAILY READING

SCHEDULE

TIME	EVENT

DAILY ACTION LIST

MOVEMENT

GOAL	ACTUAL

HYDRATION

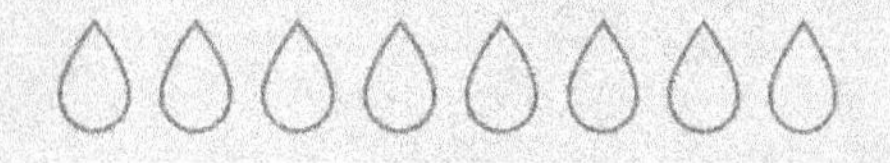

ENCOURAGE

NAME	ACTION
NAME	ACTION

SLEEP TRACKER

HOURS GOAL	ACTUAL
BEDTIME	WAKE TIME

PRAYERS FOR ME TODAY

PRAYERS FOR OTHERS TODAY

Notes

JoySoul Daily

DATE:

S M T W T F S

PRAISES

CONFESS

TOP PRIORITIES

DAILY READING

SCHEDULE

TIME	EVENT

DAILY ACTION LIST

MOVEMENT

GOAL	ACTUAL

HYDRATION

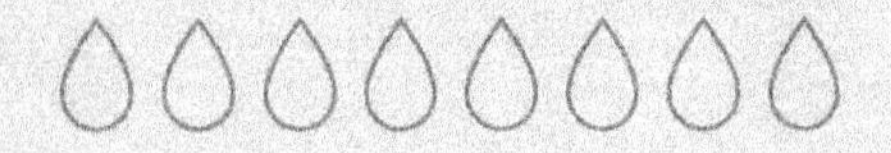

ENCOURAGE

NAME	ACTION
NAME	ACTION

SLEEP TRACKER

HOURS GOAL	ACTUAL
BEDTIME	WAKE TIME

PRAYERS FOR ME TODAY

PRAYERS FOR OTHERS TODAY

Notes

JoySoul Daily

DATE:

S M T W T F S

PRAISES

CONFESS

TOP PRIORITIES

DAILY READING

SCHEDULE

TIME	EVENT

DAILY ACTION LIST

MOVEMENT

GOAL	ACTUAL

HYDRATION

ENCOURAGE

NAME	ACTION
NAME	ACTION

SLEEP TRACKER

HOURS GOAL	ACTUAL
BEDTIME	WAKE TIME

PRAYERS FOR ME TODAY

PRAYERS FOR OTHERS TODAY

Notes

JoySoul Daily

DATE:

S M T W T F S

PRAISES

CONFESS

TOP PRIORITIES

DAILY READING

SCHEDULE

TIME	EVENT

DAILY ACTION LIST

MOVEMENT

GOAL	ACTUAL

HYDRATION

ENCOURAGE

NAME	ACTION
NAME	ACTION

SLEEP TRACKER

HOURS GOAL	ACTUAL
BEDTIME	WAKE TIME

PRAYERS FOR ME TODAY

PRAYERS FOR OTHERS TODAY

Notes

JoySoul Daily

DATE:

S M T W T F S

PRAISES

CONFESS

TOP PRIORITIES

DAILY READING

SCHEDULE

TIME	EVENT

DAILY ACTION LIST

MOVEMENT

GOAL	ACTUAL

HYDRATION

ENCOURAGE

NAME	ACTION
NAME	ACTION

SLEEP TRACKER

HOURS GOAL	ACTUAL
BEDTIME	WAKE TIME

PRAYERS FOR ME TODAY

PRAYERS FOR OTHERS TODAY

Notes

JoySoul Daily

DATE:

S M T W T F S

PRAISES

CONFESS

TOP PRIORITIES

DAILY READING

SCHEDULE

TIME	EVENT

DAILY ACTION LIST

MOVEMENT

GOAL	ACTUAL

HYDRATION

ENCOURAGE

NAME	ACTION
NAME	ACTION

SLEEP TRACKER

HOURS GOAL	ACTUAL
BEDTIME	WAKE TIME

PRAYERS FOR ME TODAY

PRAYERS FOR OTHERS TODAY

Notes

JoySoul Daily

DATE:

S M T W T F S

PRAISES

CONFESS

TOP PRIORITIES

DAILY READING

MOVEMENT

GOAL	ACTUAL

HYDRATION

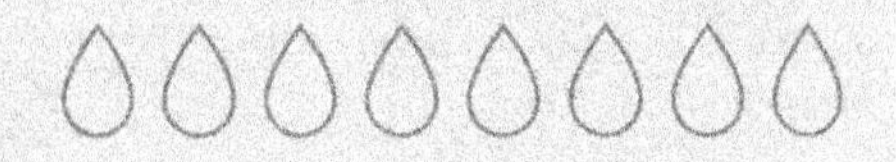

ENCOURAGE

NAME	ACTION
NAME	ACTION

SCHEDULE

TIME	EVENT

DAILY ACTION LIST

SLEEP TRACKER

HOURS GOAL	ACTUAL
BEDTIME	WAKE TIME

PRAYERS FOR ME TODAY

PRAYERS FOR OTHERS TODAY

Notes

COMMIT TO THE LORD WHATEVER YOU DO AND HE WILL ESTABLISH YOUR PLANS.

PROVERBS 16:3

THE WEEK IN REVIEW .... RATE: ☆ ☆ ☆ ☆ ☆

SABBATH DAY .... WORD OF THE WEEK ....

REFLECTION WITH THE LORD AND YOUR PRIORITIES

GOD REVEALED TO ME ....

....

THIS WEEK'S BLESSINGS ....

....

WHAT DO I NEED TO SURRENDER TO THE LORD ....

....

PRIORITY PRAYERS FOR MYSELF AND OTHERS

LOOKING AT NEXT WEEK

#1 THING TO DO NEXT ....

EXCUSE TO LET GO OF ....

I AM COMMITING TO THE LORD ....

Sermon & Journal Notes

DEVOTIONAL WEEK 8:

The Power of Prayer

"This, then, is how you should pray: 'Our Father in heaven, hallowed be your name, your kingdom come, your will be done, on earth as it is in heaven. Give us today our daily bread. And forgive us our debts, as we also have forgiven our debtors. And lead us not into temptation but deliver us from the evil one.'"

Matthew 6:9-13

Sister, there is power in your prayers!

When you are seeking to grow in your relationship with the Lord, along with reading His Word, prayer is one of the best places to start. If you're like me and sometimes struggle with perfectionism, I'm very happy to encourage you with this: *your prayers don't have to be perfect*. God isn't looking for perfection; He is looking for you to express what is in your heart. He desires a relationship with you.

In the book of Matthew, we see that even the disciples struggled with how to pray, since they asked Jesus to teach them how. After their request, Jesus taught them the Lord's Prayer.

When broken down, The Lord's Prayer offers a helpful outline that can guide us in our prayers.

Over the next several weeks, we will walk through this prayer using the acronym PRAY.

This week, I encourage you to pray the Lord's Prayer each morning as part of your morning routine.

God bless your week ahead.

God loves you. God chose you. You are His.

Love,

Your sister in Christ,

Amanda

JoySoul Daily

DATE:

S M T W T F S

PRAISES

CONFESS

TOP PRIORITIES

DAILY READING

SCHEDULE

TIME	EVENT

DAILY ACTION LIST

MOVEMENT

GOAL	ACTUAL

HYDRATION

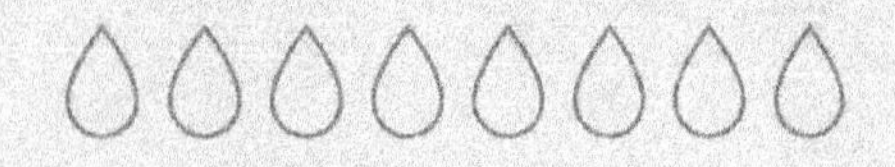

ENCOURAGE

NAME	ACTION
NAME	ACTION

SLEEP TRACKER

HOURS GOAL	ACTUAL
BEDTIME	WAKE TIME

PRAYERS FOR ME TODAY

PRAYERS FOR OTHERS TODAY

Notes

JoySoul Daily

DATE:

S M T W T F S

PRAISES

CONFESS

TOP PRIORITIES

DAILY READING

MOVEMENT

GOAL	ACTUAL

HYDRATION

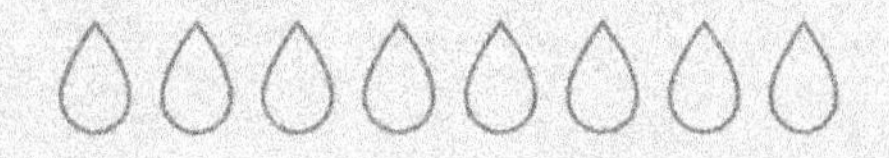

ENCOURAGE

NAME	ACTION
NAME	ACTION

SCHEDULE

TIME	EVENT

DAILY ACTION LIST

SLEEP TRACKER

HOURS GOAL	ACTUAL
BEDTIME	WAKE TIME

PRAYERS FOR ME TODAY

PRAYERS FOR OTHERS TODAY

Notes

JoySoul Daily

DATE:

S M T W T F S

PRAISES

CONFESS

TOP PRIORITIES

DAILY READING

SCHEDULE

TIME	EVENT

DAILY ACTION LIST

MOVEMENT

GOAL	ACTUAL

HYDRATION

ENCOURAGE

NAME	ACTION
NAME	ACTION

SLEEP TRACKER

HOURS GOAL	ACTUAL
BEDTIME	WAKE TIME

PRAYERS FOR ME TODAY

PRAYERS FOR OTHERS TODAY

Notes

JoySoul Daily

DATE:

S M T W T F S

PRAISES

CONFESS

TOP PRIORITIES

DAILY READING

SCHEDULE

TIME	EVENT

DAILY ACTION LIST

MOVEMENT

GOAL	ACTUAL

HYDRATION

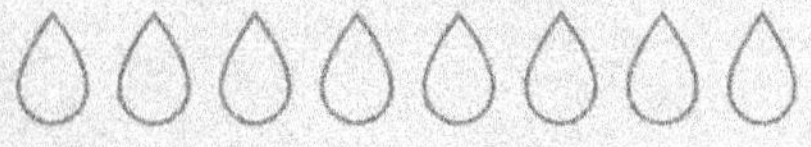

ENCOURAGE

NAME	ACTION
NAME	ACTION

SLEEP TRACKER

HOURS GOAL	ACTUAL
BEDTIME	WAKE TIME

PRAYERS FOR ME TODAY

PRAYERS FOR OTHERS TODAY

Notes

JoySoul Daily

DATE:

S M T W T F S

PRAISES

CONFESS

TOP PRIORITIES

DAILY READING

SCHEDULE

TIME	EVENT

DAILY ACTION LIST

MOVEMENT

GOAL	ACTUAL

HYDRATION

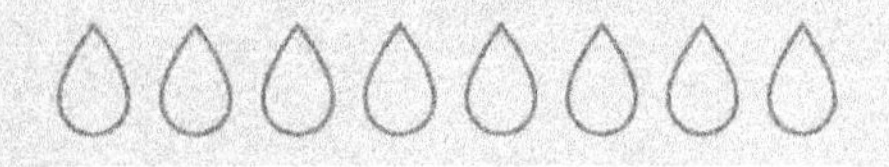

ENCOURAGE

NAME	ACTION
NAME	ACTION

SLEEP TRACKER

HOURS GOAL	ACTUAL
BEDTIME	WAKE TIME

PRAYERS FOR ME TODAY

PRAYERS FOR OTHERS TODAY

Notes

JoySoul Daily

DATE:

S M T W T F S

PRAISES

CONFESS

TOP PRIORITIES

DAILY READING

SCHEDULE

TIME	EVENT

DAILY ACTION LIST

MOVEMENT

GOAL	ACTUAL

HYDRATION

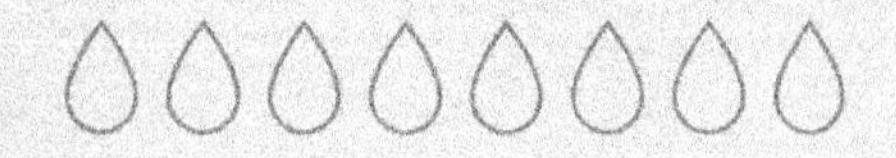

ENCOURAGE

NAME	ACTION
NAME	ACTION

SLEEP TRACKER

HOURS GOAL	ACTUAL
BEDTIME	WAKE TIME

PRAYERS FOR ME TODAY

PRAYERS FOR OTHERS TODAY

Notes

JoySoul Daily

DATE:

S M T W T F S

PRAISES

CONFESS

TOP PRIORITIES

DAILY READING

MOVEMENT

GOAL	ACTUAL

HYDRATION

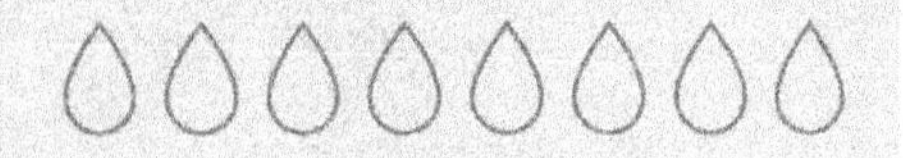

ENCOURAGE

NAME	ACTION
NAME	ACTION

SCHEDULE

TIME	EVENT

DAILY ACTION LIST

SLEEP TRACKER

HOURS GOAL	ACTUAL
BEDTIME	WAKE TIME

PRAYERS FOR ME TODAY

PRAYERS FOR OTHERS TODAY

Notes

COMMIT TO THE LORD WHATEVER YOU DO AND HE WILL ESTABLISH YOUR PLANS.

PROVERBS 16:3

THE WEEK IN REVIEW .... RATE: ☆☆☆☆☆

SABBATH DAY .... WORD OF THE WEEK ....

REFLECTION WITH THE LORD AND YOUR PRIORITIES

GOD REVEALED TO ME ....

....

THIS WEEK'S BLESSINGS ....

....

WHAT DO I NEED TO SURRENDER TO THE LORD ....

....

PRIORITY PRAYERS FOR MYSELF AND OTHERS

LOOKING AT NEXT WEEK

#1 THING TO DO NEXT ....

EXCUSE TO LET GO OF ....

I AM COMMITING TO THE LORD ....

Sermon & Journal Notes

Monthly Planner

SUN	MON	TUES	WED

"Do not conform to the pattern of this world but be transformed by the renewing of your mind. Then you will be able to test and approve what God's will is – his good, pleasing, and perfect will."

ROMANS 12:2

Month Year

THURS	FRI	SAT

Priority List

Monthly Goals

DEVOTIONAL WEEK 9:

Praise

"Our Father in heaven, hallowed be your name."

Matthew 6:9

As I mentioned in last week's devotional, there is power in your prayers. And if you are looking to grow in your relationship with the Lord, prayer is one the best places to start.

One of the first things I learned about prayer is the importance of beginning with praising the Lord. As Scripture says, every good and perfect gift comes from the Lord (James 1:17), and when we are intentional about starting our prayers with praise, we open ourselves to awareness of the good gifts God has placed in our lives.

Social media comparison traps, negative media streams, broken hearts, addiction, betrayal, grief, and all the other battles we face from living in a fallen world are tools the Devil uses to try to distract us from the good and perfect will of God.

I want to encourage you today, because it is no accident that you are reading this. God has plans for you in this season, right where you are.

Remember to start your prayers with praise, and I promise the Lord will reveal the goodness that is at work in your life and in your heart.

God bless your week ahead.

God loves you. God chose you. You are His.

Love,

your sister in Christ,

amanda

"Every good and perfect gift is from above, coming down from the Father of heavenly lights, who does not change like shifting shadows."

James 1:17 (KJV)

JoySoul Daily

DATE:

S M T W T F S

PRAISES

CONFESS

TOP PRIORITIES

DAILY READING

SCHEDULE

TIME	EVENT

DAILY ACTION LIST

MOVEMENT

GOAL	ACTUAL

HYDRATION

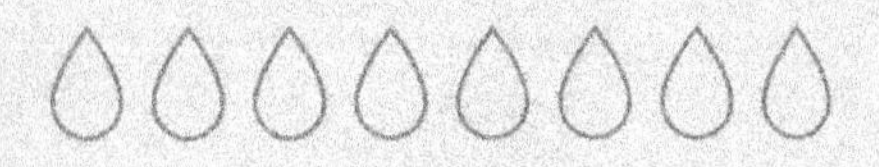

ENCOURAGE

NAME	ACTION
NAME	ACTION

SLEEP TRACKER

HOURS GOAL	ACTUAL
BEDTIME	WAKE TIME

PRAYERS FOR ME TODAY

PRAYERS FOR OTHERS TODAY

Notes

JoySoul Daily

DATE:

S M T W T F S

PRAISES

CONFESS

TOP PRIORITIES

DAILY READING

MOVEMENT

GOAL	ACTUAL

HYDRATION

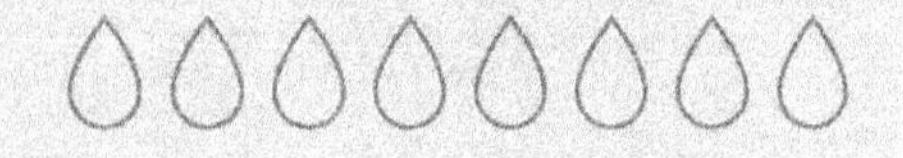

ENCOURAGE

NAME	ACTION
NAME	ACTION

SCHEDULE

TIME	EVENT

DAILY ACTION LIST

SLEEP TRACKER

HOURS GOAL	ACTUAL
BEDTIME	WAKE TIME

PRAYERS FOR ME TODAY

PRAYERS FOR OTHERS TODAY

Notes

JoySoul Daily

DATE:

S M T W T F S

PRAISES

CONFESS

TOP PRIORITIES

DAILY READING

MOVEMENT

GOAL	ACTUAL

HYDRATION

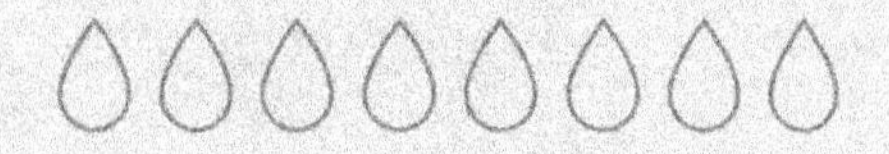

ENCOURAGE

NAME	ACTION
NAME	ACTION

SCHEDULE

TIME	EVENT

DAILY ACTION LIST

SLEEP TRACKER

HOURS GOAL	ACTUAL
BEDTIME	WAKE TIME

PRAYERS FOR ME TODAY

PRAYERS FOR OTHERS TODAY

Notes

JoySoul Daily

DATE:

S M T W T F S

PRAISES

CONFESS

TOP PRIORITIES

DAILY READING

MOVEMENT

GOAL	ACTUAL

HYDRATION

ENCOURAGE

NAME	ACTION
NAME	ACTION

SCHEDULE

TIME	EVENT

DAILY ACTION LIST

SLEEP TRACKER

HOURS GOAL	ACTUAL
BEDTIME	WAKE TIME

PRAYERS FOR ME TODAY

PRAYERS FOR OTHERS TODAY

Notes

JoySoul Daily

DATE:

S M T W T F S

PRAISES

CONFESS

TOP PRIORITIES

DAILY READING

MOVEMENT

GOAL	ACTUAL

HYDRATION

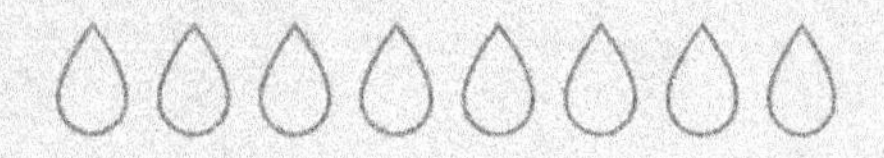

ENCOURAGE

NAME	ACTION
NAME	ACTION

SCHEDULE

TIME	EVENT

DAILY ACTION LIST

SLEEP TRACKER

HOURS GOAL	ACTUAL
BEDTIME	WAKE TIME

PRAYERS FOR ME TODAY

PRAYERS FOR OTHERS TODAY

Notes

JoySoul Daily

DATE:

S M T W T F S

PRAISES

CONFESS

TOP PRIORITIES

DAILY READING

SCHEDULE

TIME	EVENT

DAILY ACTION LIST

MOVEMENT

GOAL	ACTUAL

HYDRATION

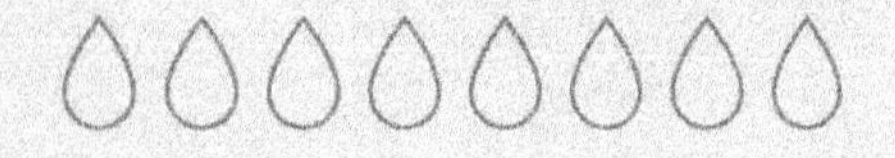

ENCOURAGE

NAME	ACTION
NAME	ACTION

SLEEP TRACKER

HOURS GOAL	ACTUAL
BEDTIME	WAKE TIME

PRAYERS FOR ME TODAY

PRAYERS FOR OTHERS TODAY

Notes

JoySoul Daily

DATE:

S M T W T F S

PRAISES

CONFESS

TOP PRIORITIES

DAILY READING

MOVEMENT

GOAL	ACTUAL

HYDRATION

ENCOURAGE

NAME	ACTION
NAME	ACTION

SCHEDULE

TIME	EVENT

DAILY ACTION LIST

SLEEP TRACKER

HOURS GOAL	ACTUAL
BEDTIME	WAKE TIME

PRAYERS FOR ME TODAY

PRAYERS FOR OTHERS TODAY

Notes

COMMIT TO THE LORD WHATEVER YOU DO AND HE WILL ESTABLISH YOUR PLANS.

PROVERBS 16:3

THE WEEK IN REVIEW ....

RATE: ☆ ☆ ☆ ☆ ☆

SABBATH DAY ....

WORD OF THE WEEK ....

REFLECTION WITH THE LORD AND YOUR PRIORITIES

GOD REVEALED TO ME ....

THIS WEEK'S BLESSINGS ....

WHAT DO I NEED TO SURRENDER TO THE LORD ....

PRIORITY PRAYERS FOR MYSELF AND OTHERS

LOOKING AT NEXT WEEK

#1 THING TO DO NEXT ....

EXCUSE TO LET GO OF ....

I AM COMMITING TO THE LORD ....

Sermon & Journal Notes

DEVOTIONAL WEEK 10:

Repent

Last week, we talked about starting our prayers with *praise*, and today I'm going to share why we should follow praise with *repentance*.

Today's word, repent, is based on the part of the Lord's Prayer that says "forgive us our debts as we forgive our debtors" (Matthew 6:12).

The Devil wants to weaken our joy, so he tries to get us to believe the lie that our sin is so bad that the Lord won't forgive us. He puts lies of shame and guilt into our thoughts.

The battle armor we have against this tactic of the enemy is the confession of our sin. Confession of our sin brings our sin out of the dark and into Lord's healing light.

If you struggle in this area, I want to encourage you to ask the Lord to help you; the Lord loves you, and you are free from the chains of your sin by the grace of Jesus' death on the cross.

Don't run away from Him, but rather confess your sin, repent, and know you are forgiven.

Then, ask the Lord to help you to not continue to sin.

Repent, and know you are loved. You are worthy.

God bless your week ahead.

God loves you. God chose you. You are His

Love.

your sister in Christ,

amanda

JoySoul Daily

DATE:

S M T W T F S

PRAISES

CONFESS

TOP PRIORITIES

DAILY READING

MOVEMENT

GOAL	ACTUAL

HYDRATION

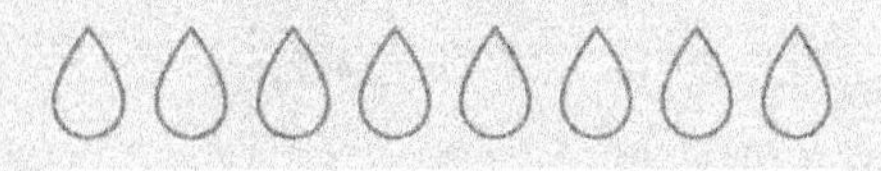

ENCOURAGE

NAME	ACTION
NAME	ACTION

SCHEDULE

TIME	EVENT

DAILY ACTION LIST

SLEEP TRACKER

HOURS GOAL	ACTUAL
BEDTIME	WAKE TIME

PRAYERS FOR ME TODAY

PRAYERS FOR OTHERS TODAY

Notes

JoySoul Daily

DATE:

S M T W T F S

PRAISES

CONFESS

TOP PRIORITIES

DAILY READING

MOVEMENT

GOAL	ACTUAL

HYDRATION

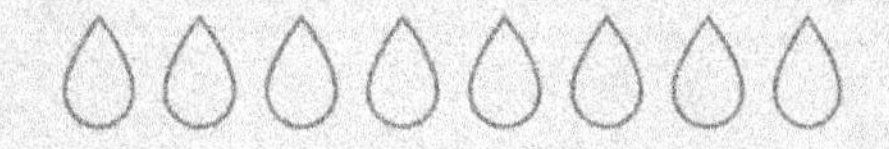

ENCOURAGE

NAME	ACTION
NAME	ACTION

SCHEDULE

TIME	EVENT

DAILY ACTION LIST

SLEEP TRACKER

HOURS GOAL	ACTUAL
BEDTIME	WAKE TIME

PRAYERS FOR ME TODAY

PRAYERS FOR OTHERS TODAY

Notes

JoySoul Daily

DATE:

S M T W T F S

PRAISES

CONFESS

TOP PRIORITIES

DAILY READING

MOVEMENT

GOAL	ACTUAL

HYDRATION

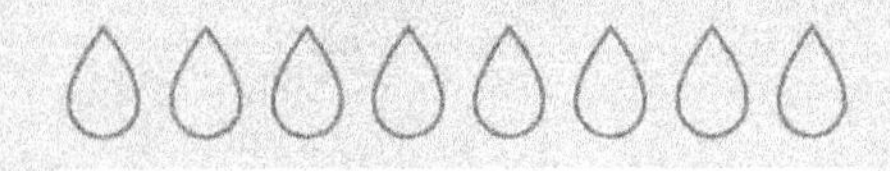

ENCOURAGE

NAME	ACTION
NAME	ACTION

SCHEDULE

TIME	EVENT

DAILY ACTION LIST

SLEEP TRACKER

HOURS GOAL	ACTUAL
BEDTIME	WAKE TIME

PRAYERS FOR ME TODAY

PRAYERS FOR OTHERS TODAY

Notes

JoySoul Daily

DATE:

S M T W T F S

PRAISES

CONFESS

TOP PRIORITIES

DAILY READING

MOVEMENT

GOAL	ACTUAL

HYDRATION

ENCOURAGE

NAME	ACTION
NAME	ACTION

SCHEDULE

TIME	EVENT

DAILY ACTION LIST

SLEEP TRACKER

HOURS GOAL	ACTUAL
BEDTIME	WAKE TIME

PRAYERS FOR ME TODAY

PRAYERS FOR OTHERS TODAY

Notes

JoySoul Daily

DATE:

S M T W T F S

PRAISES

CONFESS

TOP PRIORITIES

DAILY READING

SCHEDULE

TIME	EVENT

DAILY ACTION LIST

MOVEMENT

GOAL	ACTUAL

HYDRATION

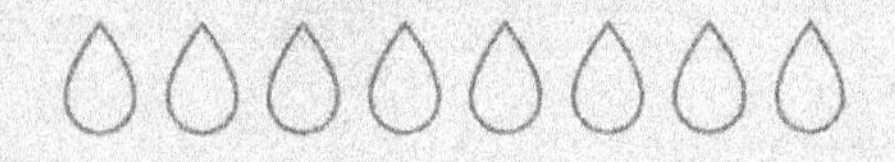

ENCOURAGE

NAME	ACTION
NAME	ACTION

SLEEP TRACKER

HOURS GOAL	ACTUAL
BEDTIME	WAKE TIME

PRAYERS FOR ME TODAY

PRAYERS FOR OTHERS TODAY

Notes

JoySoul Daily

DATE:

S M T W T F S

PRAISES

CONFESS

TOP PRIORITIES

DAILY READING

MOVEMENT

GOAL	ACTUAL

HYDRATION

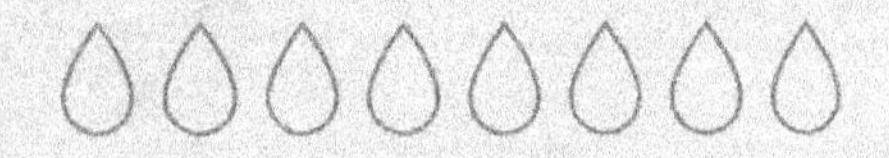

ENCOURAGE

NAME	ACTION
NAME	ACTION

SCHEDULE

TIME	EVENT

DAILY ACTION LIST

SLEEP TRACKER

HOURS GOAL	ACTUAL
BEDTIME	WAKE TIME

PRAYERS FOR ME TODAY

PRAYERS FOR OTHERS TODAY

Notes

JoySoul Daily

DATE:

S M T W T F S

PRAISES

CONFESS

TOP PRIORITIES

DAILY READING

SCHEDULE

TIME	EVENT

DAILY ACTION LIST

MOVEMENT

GOAL	ACTUAL

HYDRATION

ENCOURAGE

NAME	ACTION
NAME	ACTION

SLEEP TRACKER

HOURS GOAL	ACTUAL
BEDTIME	WAKE TIME

PRAYERS FOR ME TODAY

PRAYERS FOR OTHERS TODAY

Notes

COMMIT TO THE LORD WHATEVER YOU DO AND HE WILL ESTABLISH YOUR PLANS.

PROVERBS 16:3

THE WEEK IN REVIEW .... RATE: ☆☆☆☆☆

SABBATH DAY .... WORD OF THE WEEK ....

REFLECTION WITH THE LORD AND YOUR PRIORITIES

GOD REVEALED TO ME ....

THIS WEEK'S BLESSINGS ....

WHAT DO I NEED TO SURRENDER TO THE LORD ....

PRIORITY PRAYERS FOR MYSELF AND OTHERS

LOOKING AT NEXT WEEK

#1 THING TO DO NEXT ....

EXCUSE TO LET GO OF ....

I AM COMMITING TO THE LORD ....

Sermon & Journal Notes

DEVOTIONAL WEEK 11:

Ask

"Give us this day our daily bread.... And do not lead us into temptation but deliver us from evil."

Matthew 6:11,13

This week's word and the next step in our prayer outline is *ask*.

The Lord is our provider and knows exactly what we need. However, as relational beings, we have an innate desire to know we are loved and cared for.

When we come to God, in expectant faith that we can trust Him with our needs, we please the Lord, and He blesses us by fulfilling our desire to feel loved and cared for.

This time in prayer is your time to bring your needs and requests to the Lord.

This is also a time to pray for your family, friends, leaders, and, yes, even your enemies.

Ask in expectant faith.

God bless your week ahead.

God loves you. God chose you. You are His.

Love,

your sister in Christ,

amanda

JoySoul Daily

DATE:

S M T W T F S

PRAISES

CONFESS

TOP PRIORITIES

DAILY READING

SCHEDULE

TIME	EVENT

DAILY ACTION LIST

MOVEMENT

GOAL	ACTUAL

HYDRATION

ENCOURAGE

NAME	ACTION
NAME	ACTION

SLEEP TRACKER

HOURS GOAL	ACTUAL
BEDTIME	WAKE TIME

PRAYERS FOR ME TODAY

PRAYERS FOR OTHERS TODAY

Notes

JoySoul Daily

DATE:

S M T W T F S

PRAISES

CONFESS

TOP PRIORITIES

DAILY READING

MOVEMENT

GOAL	ACTUAL

HYDRATION

ENCOURAGE

NAME	ACTION
NAME	ACTION

SCHEDULE

TIME	EVENT

DAILY ACTION LIST

SLEEP TRACKER

HOURS GOAL	ACTUAL
BEDTIME	WAKE TIME

PRAYERS FOR ME TODAY

PRAYERS FOR OTHERS TODAY

Notes

JoySoul Daily

DATE:

S M T W T F S

PRAISES

CONFESS

TOP PRIORITIES

DAILY READING

SCHEDULE

TIME	EVENT

DAILY ACTION LIST

MOVEMENT

GOAL	ACTUAL

HYDRATION

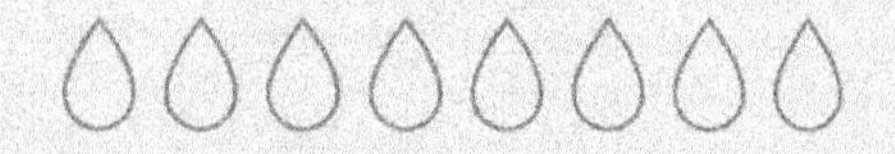

ENCOURAGE

NAME	ACTION
NAME	ACTION

SLEEP TRACKER

HOURS GOAL	ACTUAL
BEDTIME	WAKE TIME

PRAYERS FOR ME TODAY

PRAYERS FOR OTHERS TODAY

Notes

JoySoul Daily

DATE:

S M T W T F S

PRAISES

CONFESS

TOP PRIORITIES

DAILY READING

SCHEDULE

TIME	EVENT

DAILY ACTION LIST

MOVEMENT

GOAL	ACTUAL

HYDRATION

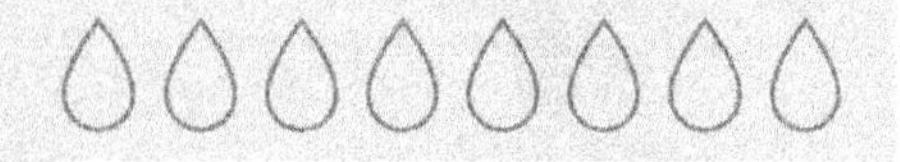

ENCOURAGE

NAME	ACTION
NAME	ACTION

SLEEP TRACKER

HOURS GOAL	ACTUAL
BEDTIME	WAKE TIME

PRAYERS FOR ME TODAY

PRAYERS FOR OTHERS TODAY

Notes

JoySoul Daily

DATE:

S M T W T F S

PRAISES

CONFESS

TOP PRIORITIES

DAILY READING

SCHEDULE

TIME	EVENT

DAILY ACTION LIST

MOVEMENT

GOAL	ACTUAL

HYDRATION

ENCOURAGE

NAME	ACTION
NAME	ACTION

SLEEP TRACKER

HOURS GOAL	ACTUAL
BEDTIME	WAKE TIME

PRAYERS FOR ME TODAY

PRAYERS FOR OTHERS TODAY

Notes

JoySoul Daily

DATE:

S M T W T F S

PRAISES

CONFESS

TOP PRIORITIES

DAILY READING

SCHEDULE

TIME	EVENT

DAILY ACTION LIST

MOVEMENT

GOAL	ACTUAL

HYDRATION

ENCOURAGE

NAME	ACTION
NAME	ACTION

SLEEP TRACKER

HOURS GOAL	ACTUAL
BEDTIME	WAKE TIME

PRAYERS FOR ME TODAY

PRAYERS FOR OTHERS TODAY

Notes

JoySoul Daily

DATE:

S M T W T F S

PRAISES

CONFESS

TOP PRIORITIES

DAILY READING

SCHEDULE

TIME	EVENT

DAILY ACTION LIST

MOVEMENT

GOAL	ACTUAL

HYDRATION

ENCOURAGE

NAME	ACTION
NAME	ACTION

SLEEP TRACKER

HOURS GOAL	ACTUAL
BEDTIME	WAKE TIME

PRAYERS FOR ME TODAY

PRAYERS FOR OTHERS TODAY

Notes

COMMIT TO THE LORD WHATEVER YOU DO AND HE WILL ESTABLISH YOUR PLANS.

PROVERBS 16:3

THE WEEK IN REVIEW .... RATE: ☆☆☆☆☆

SABBATH DAY .... WORD OF THE WEEK ....

REFLECTION WITH THE LORD AND YOUR PRIORITIES

GOD REVEALED TO ME ....

....

THIS WEEK'S BLESSINGS ....

....

WHAT DO I NEED TO SURRENDER TO THE LORD ....

....

PRIORITY PRAYERS FOR MYSELF AND OTHERS

LOOKING AT NEXT WEEK

#1 THING TO DO NEXT ....

EXCUSE TO LET GO OF ....

I AM COMMITING TO THE LORD ....

Sermon & Journal Notes

DEVOTIONAL WEEK 12:

Yield

"Your kingdom come. Your will be done, on earth as it is in heaven."

Matthew 6:10

When we pray, sometimes we can get so caught up in our current circumstances that we lose sight of the purpose of prayer. I thought Craig Groeschel described this perfectly on Twitter when he said, "The purpose of prayer isn't to get God to do our will. The purpose of prayer is to know God so we can do His will" (Groeschel 2022).

Before I rededicated my life to Christ, I was up and down in my relationship with the Lord because I wasn't consistent in my time with Him and in His Word. This led me to quickly lose trust in Him and to take matters into my own hands instead of waiting on Him. This caused me so much stress, regret, and disappointment.

All that to say, such beautiful blessings come into your life when you yield to His will instead of trying to convince Him to do yours.

I'm so thankful I can trust Him fully to work in my life, and, sister, you can too.

Praise. Repent. Ask. Yield.

God bless your week ahead.

God loves you. God chose you. You are His.

Love,
your sister in Christ,
amanda

JoySoul Daily

DATE:

S M T W T F S

PRAISES

CONFESS

TOP PRIORITIES

DAILY READING

MOVEMENT

GOAL	ACTUAL

HYDRATION

ENCOURAGE

NAME	ACTION
NAME	ACTION

SCHEDULE

TIME	EVENT

DAILY ACTION LIST

SLEEP TRACKER

HOURS GOAL	ACTUAL
BEDTIME	WAKE TIME

PRAYERS FOR ME TODAY

PRAYERS FOR OTHERS TODAY

Notes

JoySoul Daily

DATE:

S M T W T F S

PRAISES

CONFESS

TOP PRIORITIES

DAILY READING

MOVEMENT

GOAL	ACTUAL

HYDRATION

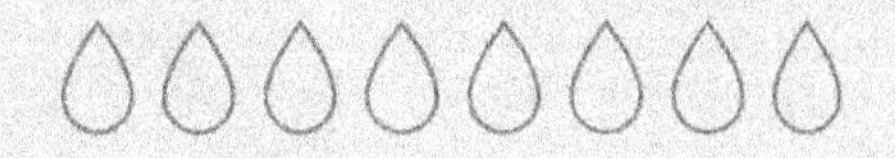

ENCOURAGE

NAME	ACTION
NAME	ACTION

SCHEDULE

TIME	EVENT

DAILY ACTION LIST

SLEEP TRACKER

HOURS GOAL	ACTUAL
BEDTIME	WAKE TIME

PRAYERS FOR ME TODAY

PRAYERS FOR OTHERS TODAY

Notes

JoySoul Daily

DATE:

S M T W T F S

PRAISES

CONFESS

TOP PRIORITIES

DAILY READING

SCHEDULE

TIME	EVENT

DAILY ACTION LIST

MOVEMENT

GOAL	ACTUAL

HYDRATION

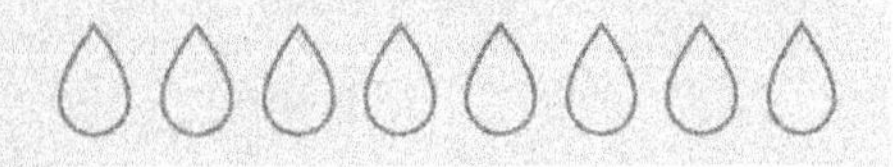

ENCOURAGE

NAME	ACTION
NAME	ACTION

SLEEP TRACKER

HOURS GOAL	ACTUAL
BEDTIME	WAKE TIME

PRAYERS FOR ME TODAY

PRAYERS FOR OTHERS TODAY

Notes

JoySoul Daily

DATE:

S M T W T F S

PRAISES

CONFESS

TOP PRIORITIES

DAILY READING

SCHEDULE

TIME	EVENT

DAILY ACTION LIST

MOVEMENT

GOAL	ACTUAL

HYDRATION

ENCOURAGE

NAME	ACTION
NAME	ACTION

SLEEP TRACKER

HOURS GOAL	ACTUAL
BEDTIME	WAKE TIME

PRAYERS FOR ME TODAY

PRAYERS FOR OTHERS TODAY

Notes

JoySoul Daily

DATE:

S M T W T F S

PRAISES

CONFESS

TOP PRIORITIES

DAILY READING

SCHEDULE

TIME	EVENT

DAILY ACTION LIST

MOVEMENT

GOAL	ACTUAL

HYDRATION

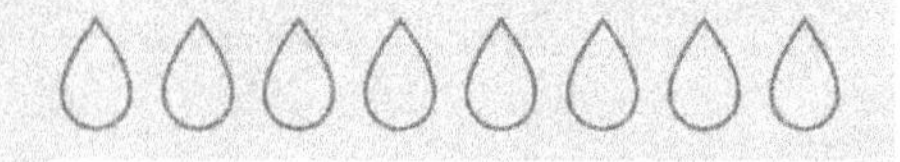

ENCOURAGE

NAME	ACTION
NAME	ACTION

SLEEP TRACKER

HOURS GOAL	ACTUAL
BEDTIME	WAKE TIME

PRAYERS FOR ME TODAY

PRAYERS FOR OTHERS TODAY

Notes

JoySoul Daily

DATE:

S M T W T F S

PRAISES

CONFESS

TOP PRIORITIES

DAILY READING

SCHEDULE

TIME	EVENT

DAILY ACTION LIST

MOVEMENT

GOAL	ACTUAL

HYDRATION

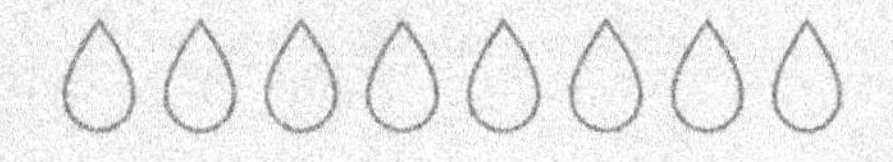

ENCOURAGE

NAME	ACTION
NAME	ACTION

SLEEP TRACKER

HOURS GOAL	ACTUAL
BEDTIME	WAKE TIME

PRAYERS FOR ME TODAY

PRAYERS FOR OTHERS TODAY

Notes

JoySoul Daily

DATE:

S M T W T F S

PRAISES

CONFESS

TOP PRIORITIES

DAILY READING

SCHEDULE

TIME	EVENT

DAILY ACTION LIST

MOVEMENT

GOAL	ACTUAL

HYDRATION

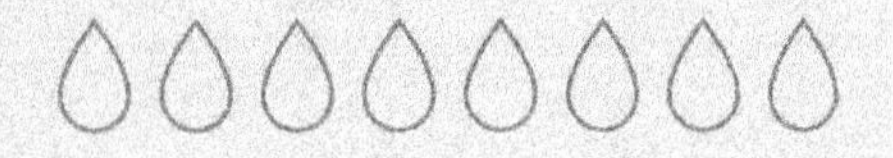

ENCOURAGE

NAME	ACTION
NAME	ACTION

SLEEP TRACKER

HOURS GOAL	ACTUAL
BEDTIME	WAKE TIME

PRAYERS FOR ME TODAY

PRAYERS FOR OTHERS TODAY

Notes

COMMIT TO THE LORD WHATEVER YOU DO AND HE WILL ESTABLISH YOUR PLANS.

PROVERBS 16:3

THE WEEK IN REVIEW .... RATE: ☆☆☆☆☆

SABBATH DAY .... WORD OF THE WEEK ....

REFLECTION WITH THE LORD AND YOUR PRIORITIES

GOD REVEALED TO ME ....

....

THIS WEEK'S BLESSINGS ....

....

WHAT DO I NEED TO SURRENDER TO THE LORD ....

....

PRIORITY PRAYERS FOR MYSELF AND OTHERS

LOOKING AT NEXT WEEK

#1 THING TO DO NEXT ....

EXCUSE TO LET GO OF ....

I AM COMMITING TO THE LORD ....

Sermon & Journal Notes

DEVOTIONAL WEEK 13:

A Holy Spirit-Transformed, Faith-Filled JoySoul!

"'Don't be afraid,' the prophet answered. 'Those who are with us are more than those who are with them.' And Elisha prayed, 'Open his eyes, Lord, so that he may see.' Then the Lord opened the servant's eyes, and he looked and saw the hills full of horses and chariots of fire all around Elisha."

2 Kings 6:16-17

You are a warrior; a Holy Spirit-transformed, faith-filled *JoySoul*!

As Christian women, how we see the natural doesn't represent what surrounds us in the spiritual realm. When we arm ourselves every day with prayer, trust, and time in the Lord's Word, we cover ourselves with spiritual armor. The Holy Spirit's power is at work inside of us and we can trust in the Lord to get us through any situation.

I love Second Kings 6:8-24. This is a story about the unshakable faith and generosity of the prophet Elisha. It provides us with an example of just how powerful trust and faith in the Lord can be.

In this story, the Syrian army was on the attack against Israel. Fortunately, Elisha listened to the Lord and was able to help the Israeli army escape the attacks. The Syrian king was outraged; he thought there was a spy in his army telling the Israelites exactly how to escape their attacks. His army told them about Elisha, how he knew exactly what their plans were, and that he was the one telling the king of Israel how to escape from them.

The king of Syria then ordered his men to capture Elisha

and bring him back to him. When the army arrived at Elisha's home, his servant was terrified, but Elisha prayed that the Lord would open his servant's eyes so that he could see the thousands of angels and chariots that were there protecting them. As the Syrian army got closer, Elisha prayed for the Lord to blind their eyes, and then told them to follow him; he would take them to the man they were looking for. He then led them to the king of Israel. When they arrived, Elisha prayed that the Lord would remove the blindness from their eyes. When their sight was restored, they were quickly struck with fear, as they knew the king of Israel would have them killed. The Israeli king then asked Elisha if he should kill them. Elisha said not to kill them, but to give them food and drink, and then send them back to the king of Syria. The king did as Elisha suggested, and when the army was sent back, the king of Syria decided to no longer attack Israel.

This story made me think of a couple of takeaways for our own lives today. When you have faith and trust in the Lord, He will protect you and guide you. You will be able to see with faith-filled eyes and not be distracted by fear.

With that in mind, my prayer for you is that you would face each new day with courage and faith, because through the power of the Holy Spirit, you can defeat any evil army that comes against you in Jesus' name!

God bless your week ahead.

God loves you. God chose you. You are His.

Love,

your sister in Christ,

amanda

JoySoul Daily

DATE:

S M T W T F S

PRAISES

CONFESS

TOP PRIORITIES

DAILY READING

SCHEDULE

TIME	EVENT

DAILY ACTION LIST

MOVEMENT

GOAL	ACTUAL

HYDRATION

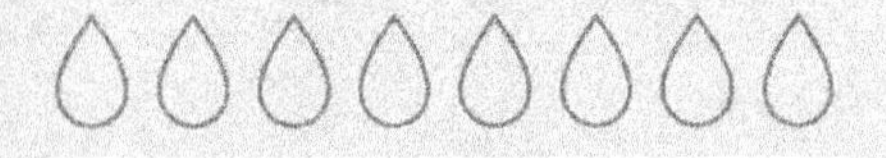

ENCOURAGE

NAME	ACTION
NAME	ACTION

SLEEP TRACKER

HOURS GOAL	ACTUAL
BEDTIME	WAKE TIME

PRAYERS FOR ME TODAY

PRAYERS FOR OTHERS TODAY

Notes

JoySoul Daily

DATE:

S M T W T F S

PRAISES

CONFESS

TOP PRIORITIES

DAILY READING

SCHEDULE

TIME	EVENT

DAILY ACTION LIST

MOVEMENT

GOAL	ACTUAL

HYDRATION

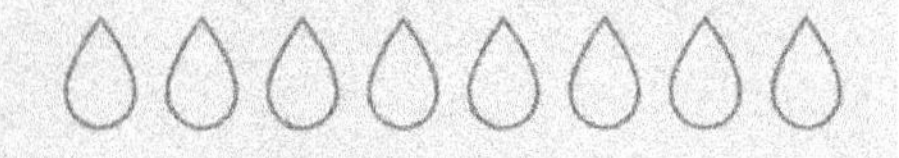

ENCOURAGE

NAME	ACTION
NAME	ACTION

SLEEP TRACKER

HOURS GOAL	ACTUAL
BEDTIME	WAKE TIME

PRAYERS FOR ME TODAY

PRAYERS FOR OTHERS TODAY

Notes

JoySoul Daily

DATE:

S M T W T F S

PRAISES

CONFESS

TOP PRIORITIES

DAILY READING

SCHEDULE

TIME	EVENT

DAILY ACTION LIST

MOVEMENT

GOAL	ACTUAL

HYDRATION

ENCOURAGE

NAME	ACTION
NAME	ACTION

SLEEP TRACKER

HOURS GOAL	ACTUAL
BEDTIME	WAKE TIME

PRAYERS FOR ME TODAY

PRAYERS FOR OTHERS TODAY

Notes

JoySoul Daily

DATE:

S M T W T F S

PRAISES

CONFESS

TOP PRIORITIES

DAILY READING

SCHEDULE

TIME	EVENT

DAILY ACTION LIST

MOVEMENT

GOAL	ACTUAL

HYDRATION

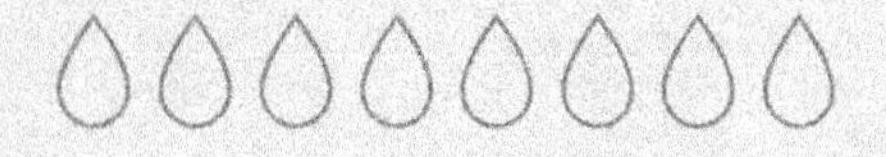

ENCOURAGE

NAME	ACTION
NAME	ACTION

SLEEP TRACKER

HOURS GOAL	ACTUAL
BEDTIME	WAKE TIME

PRAYERS FOR ME TODAY

PRAYERS FOR OTHERS TODAY

Notes

JoySoul Daily

DATE:

S M T W T F S

PRAISES

CONFESS

TOP PRIORITIES

DAILY READING

MOVEMENT

GOAL	ACTUAL

HYDRATION

ENCOURAGE

NAME	ACTION
NAME	ACTION

SCHEDULE

TIME	EVENT

DAILY ACTION LIST

SLEEP TRACKER

HOURS GOAL	ACTUAL
BEDTIME	WAKE TIME

PRAYERS FOR ME TODAY

PRAYERS FOR OTHERS TODAY

Notes

JoySoul Daily

DATE:

S M T W T F S

PRAISES

CONFESS

TOP PRIORITIES

DAILY READING

SCHEDULE

TIME	EVENT

DAILY ACTION LIST

MOVEMENT

GOAL	ACTUAL

HYDRATION

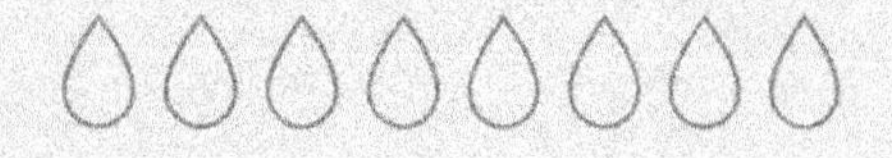

ENCOURAGE

NAME	ACTION
NAME	ACTION

SLEEP TRACKER

HOURS GOAL	ACTUAL
BEDTIME	WAKE TIME

PRAYERS FOR ME TODAY

PRAYERS FOR OTHERS TODAY

Notes

JoySoul Daily

DATE:

S M T W T F S

PRAISES

CONFESS

TOP PRIORITIES

DAILY READING

MOVEMENT

GOAL	ACTUAL

HYDRATION

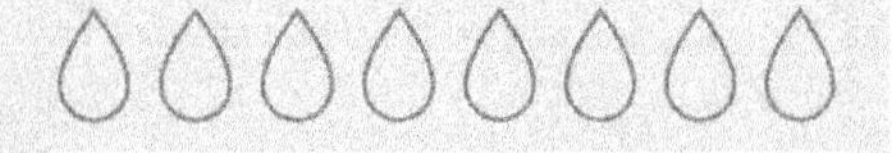

ENCOURAGE

NAME	ACTION
NAME	ACTION

SCHEDULE

TIME	EVENT

DAILY ACTION LIST

SLEEP TRACKER

HOURS GOAL	ACTUAL
BEDTIME	WAKE TIME

PRAYERS FOR ME TODAY

PRAYERS FOR OTHERS TODAY

Notes

COMMIT TO THE LORD WHATEVER YOU DO AND HE WILL ESTABLISH YOUR PLANS.

PROVERBS 16:3

THE WEEK IN REVIEW .... RATE: ☆☆☆☆☆

SABBATH DAY .... WORD OF THE WEEK ....

REFLECTION WITH THE LORD AND YOUR PRIORITIES

GOD REVEALED TO ME ....

....

THIS WEEK'S BLESSINGS ....

....

WHAT DO I NEED TO SURRENDER TO THE LORD ....

....

PRIORITY PRAYERS FOR MYSELF AND OTHERS

LOOKING AT NEXT WEEK

#1 THING TO DO NEXT ....

EXCUSE TO LET GO OF ....

I AM COMMITING TO THE LORD ....

Sermon & Journal Notes

JoySoul Planner Reflection

How has this journey through the thirteen-week *JoySoul Connection* transformed your prayer life?

How has the *JoySoul Connection Planner* improved your awareness of the Lord?

How have you used the *JoySoul Connection Planner* to minister to others?

Lord, I pray a blessing over this JoySoul. *The world needs the special gifts and talents you have blessed her with. Lord, I pray that you would give her the courage, desire, and ability to walk in expectant faith and live out your mission and purpose in her life. I pray this over her in Jesus' name, Amen.*

God loves you. God chose you. You are His.

Love,

your sister in Christ,

amanda

Resources: My Faith Favorites

The Bible Recap Chronological 1 Year Bible Reading Plan

Visit thebiblerecap.com/start for everything you will need to know about how to get started.

The Bible Recap Podcast

In this podcast, Tara-Leigh Cobble provides a brief commentary for each day of the Bible reading plan

DGroup

This Bible study group has helped me remain accountable to consistently reading God's Word and has blessed my life with the most amazing prayer warriors and friendships. For more information or to join a DGroup, visit www.mydgroup.org/start.

UVersion Bible App

A full-service resource with access to the Bible, devotional plans, prayers, and much more.

Echo App

A free phone app that helps you pray. You can remind yourself to pray for specific people or topics, and you can ask others to pray for you.

The Bible Project App

This phone app provides tons of resources, including beautiful visuals, commentaries, and podcasts, that can help you on your journey of understanding the Bible and growing in your relationship with the Lord.

Blended Kingdom Families

A stepfamily ministry that serves to spread the gospel to blended families all over the world and help shine the light of Jesus into every home and marriage. They recently released a book called Blended & Redeemed: The Go-To Field Guide for the Modern Stepfamily. My husband and I have been married ten years at the writing of this devotional planner, and I would have loved to have their resources when I was a single mother and when Jason and I were dating. And their book has already blessed us even at this current stage of our marriage. For any of you that are currently single parents, in a blended family, or have close friends/family that are, I highly recommend their book and ministry resources. You can find more information on their website: https://blendedkingdomfamilies.com/

***JoySoul Connection* Daily Encouragement**

Website: joysoulconnection.com
Facebook group: https://www.facebook.com/groups/2286818411448254
Linked-In: www.linkedin.com/company/joysoul-corporation
Instagram: @joysoulconnection

Resources: My Health and Lifestyle Favorites

My Fitness Pal Exercise and Food Tracker

The *My Fitness Pal* app allows you to track your meals, macros, calories, nutrition, etc. I wasn't born with that intuitive eating brain signal (I love to eat!), so this tool has been vital for me with weight loss and portion control.

Hydration

Water is so important! What has helped me stay hydrated has been filling up my 72-ounce water jug at the start of my day, and then use it to fill up my 32-ounce Yeti until it's gone. This has kept me on track with my daily hydration goal. Your *JoySoul* daily page includes a water tracker to celebrate each day's progress.

Sleep Tracker

My Fitbit tracker helps me track sleep patterns and quality. Here are some additional sleep apps that were top-rated in 2022: Sleep Cycle, SleepScore, Headspace, Calm, Pillow, Loona, Breathwrk, Sleepa, and Sleepzy. Your *JoySoul* daily page also includes a sleep tracker to celebrate your progress and help you set bedtime and waketime routines that work for your daily schedule.

Family Scheduler

My husband and I have been using the COZI app for our family scheduler. This app allows us to put all our events in one calendar and sends us each a weekly email, so we both know what each other has coming up in the week ahead. It also includes the ability to add your child's school calendar events, shared grocery lists, and shared to-do lists. You can also create your own "shared list," and it includes recipes.

SMART Goal Setting

Check out the following articles for further information about SMART goals:
https://www.mindtools.com/pages/article/smart-goals.htm
https://www.oberlo.com/blog/smart-goal-examples

Bibliography

Covey, Stephen R. 1989. *The 7 Habits of Highly Effective People: Powerful Lessons in Personal Change*. London: Simon and Schuster.

Groeschel, Craig. Twitter Post. May 5, 2022. https://twitter.com/craiggroeschel.

Lucado, Max. "The Power of Encouragement". Max Lucado. https://maxlucado.com/watch/power-of-encouragement/ (Accessed October 25, 2022).

About the Author

Hi! My name is Amanda Lingle. I'm so glad you're here, and I'm incredibly honored the Lord has led you to this ninety-day journey through the *JoySoul Connection Devotional Planner.*

I wanted to share a few more details with you about me and about how JoySoul Connection was placed on my heart. I'm a wife to my second chance at love, Jason, a mom to Bradyn, a bonus mom to Dylan, and I have three sweet, rambunctious dogs, Luke, Lilly, and Ella. My most cherished time is that spent with the Lord, with my family, and with my close friends.

So how did JoySoul Connection Begin? In 2020, I had a dramatic encounter with the Lord that led me on a journey of tests, trials, and ultimately to a commitment to trust and be obedient to the Lord's plan for me.

The most impactful part of this journey was the intentional time I spent getting to know the Lord by spending time in His Word and in prayer every day. I made the commitment to read the Bible within one year, and I stopped "looking for myself" and started "looking for the Lord." These practices literally transformed my heart and my life.

The Lord brought me the vision for JoySoul Connection through His Word. John 15:5 sparked a desire in my heart to help women get out of the enemy's trap of distraction and begin living their lives with God-given purpose. I now know this is part of my purpose.

I've always loved both planners and devotionals, so this devotional planner has truly been such a joy and labor of love to create. The Lord even told me, "Amanda, I know you love planners, and I want you to create one for my chosen." I was so happy to say "yes, Lord!"

In this devotional planner, I share my transformation story and provide daily templates to help you structure your quiet time, steward your body, and set your intentions with the Lord--

getting you into those healthy habits! I've also included Sunday sermon notes pages and weekly reflection pages. The thirteen weeks of devotionals include guides for how to be on guard, as well as tips for how to grow in your own understanding of and relationship with the Lord.

As you utilize the JoySoul Devotional Planner, I pray that the Lord will give you wisdom, knowledge and understanding regarding the special purpose He has just for you.

God loves you. God chose you. You are His.

Love,
your sister in Christ,
amanda

CPSIA information can be obtained
at www.ICGtesting.com
Printed in the USA
BVHW021908240323
661105BV00003B/5

9 798887 3839